Kerry Bretherton KC is a silk at 39 Essex Chambers. She specialises in property, including applications under the Electronic Communications Code, property development, building safety and related commercial transactions. She deals with all aspects of development work, real property and commercial and residential landlord and tenant for a variety of clients including developers, companies, solicitors, central and local government and private individuals by way of direct access instruction. Kerry has appeared in many of the leading property cases in the Court of Appeal and Supreme Court. Kerry is ranked in Chambers & Partners and Legal 500 and was nominated for Legal 500 Property Litigation Silk of the Year in 2022.

James Castle is a barrister at Tanfield Chambers who specialises in property litigation. This includes real property disputes, the law of landlord and tenant (both commercial and residential), and of course the Electronic Communications Code. And because property cases often involve other elements, James also regularly deals with commercial debts, insolvency issues, company law and even harassment. James also contributes to the leading legal textbook on property management.

Mark Loveday is a senior member of the property team at Tanfield Chambers, and editor of the leading legal textbook on property management. He has represented commercial and residential landlords and leaseholders at every level, including the First-tier Tribunal (Property Chamber), Upper Tribunal (Lands Chamber), Court of Appeal and Supreme Court. Mark is a judge of the First-tier Tribunal and is a member of the Tribunal Procedure Committee, responsible for writing the procedure rules for the First-tier and Upper Tribunal. His advice column on residential property matters appears in the Times property section every Friday.

The Electronic Communications Code: A Practical Guide

Second Edition

The Electronic Communications Code: A Practical Guide

Second Edition

Kerry Bretherton KC
Barrister, 39 Essex Chambers
BA (Hons)

James Castle
Barrister, Tanfield Chambers
BA (Hons) (Oxon)

Mark Loveday
Barrister, Tanfield Chambers
BA (Hons) FCIArb FIRPM

Law Brief Publishing

Published 2023 by Law Brief Publishing, an imprint of Law Brief Publishing Ltd
30 The Parks
Minehead
Somerset
TA24 8BT

www.lawbriefpublishing.com

Paperback: 978-1-914608-94-0

For our grandfathers:
Fred Wakeling (Kerry's grandad) and
Leslie Castle (James's grandpa),
without whom this book would never have been written
We owe our careers at the Bar to each of you

To Edward, Edwina and everyone in the village
(from Mark)

PREFACE

We have written this book on the new Electronic Communications Code ("**the Code**") to serve both as a first port of call for practitioners new to the regime, and as a useful reference point for those familiar with the regime.

Our focus has been primarily on those parts of the Code that are most likely to come up in practice, rather than on creating a comprehensive guide to every aspect of the Code. But this does not mean that this will be a purely whistle-stop tour. Due consideration is given to the various complexities of the new regime, especially in the context of the substantial consideration of the Code by the courts since it came into force and recent amendment to its content, some of which is yet to come into force.

We outline the parts of the Code that fall within the scope of this book and those that do not in Chapter One: An Introduction to the Electronic Communications Code. This first chapter also contains a section on the Operation and Content of the Code and this Book.

It should be noted that whilst parts of the Code do apply to other jurisdictions, this book primarily deals with how it applies in England and Wales.

The law is correct as at 1 March 2023.

Kerry Bretherton KC
Barrister, 39 Essex Chambers

Mark Loveday
Barrister, Tanfield Chambers

James Castle
Barrister, Tanfield Chambers

March 2023

CONTENTS

TABLE OF CASES

TABLE OF STATUTES

TABLE OF STATUTORY INSTRUMENTS

CHAPTER ONE

AN INTRODUCTION TO THE ELECTRONIC COMMUNICATIONS CODE

This introductory chapter deals with the following topics:

(1) The development of the Electronic Communications Code 2017 (**"the Code"**)[1] to replace the old Electronic Communications Code (**"the Old Code"**);[2]

(2) The purpose of the Code; and

(3) An overview of how the Code operates, and its contents.

The Development of the Code

Electronic communications (**"telecoms"**) infrastructure is the beating heart of modern society in our digital age. This has never been truer than in the wake of the Coronavirus pandemic, which prompted developed countries across the world to adapt to socially distanced life by embracing new remote means of communication. The United Kingdom's telecoms apparatus is now relied upon heavily not just in our homes and businesses, but also by HM Courts & Tribunals Service, the National Health Service and even our schools.

---

[1] The Code can be found set out as Schedule 3A of the Communications Act 2003, and was inserted there by Section 4(2) and Schedule 1 of the Digital Economy Act 2017.

[2] The Old Code was contained at Schedule 2 to the Telecommunications Act 1984, but is now repealed.

The technology involved in maintaining these services develops at an alarming rate; as a result, electronic data transmission rates have been growing exponentially for decades. This is one of the reasons why the statutory regime governing the relationships in the United Kingdom between its telecoms network operators and the landowners on whose land they erect their telecoms apparatus ought to be regularly reviewed and updated.

But until 28 December 2017, the United Kingdom was still using its original telecoms code, the Old Code set out in Schedule 2 to the Telecommunications Act 1984. A code, drafted before the invention of the World Wide Web, that it was envisaged would regulate the rollout of landline telephones across the United Kingdom.[3] Its draftsmen could barely have conceived of fibre-optic broadband or the 5G mobile network.

However, when the Law Commission published its independent review of the Old Code on 28 February 2013, its reasons for recommending reform were not limited to simply future proofing the existing statutory regime against emerging technologies.[4] The Law Commission recognised that the Old Code has been condemned judicially as *"not one of Parliament's better drafting efforts… one of the least coherent and thought-through pieces of legislation on the statute book"*,[5] and recommended extensive reforms to (inexhaustibly):

(1) Clarify the valuation principles for determining the consideration that landowners can charge telecoms network operators for the use of their land to host telecoms apparatus;

---

3   Albeit that it was substantially amended with effect from 25 July 2003 by Schedule 3 of the Communications Act 2003 to (1) comply with five Directives issued by the European Union and (2) reflect some developments in technology.

4   The Law Commission, *The Electronic Communications Code* (LAW COM No 336).

5   *Geo Networks Ltd v The Bridgewater Canal Company Ltd* [2010] 1 WLR 2576 at [7], by Lewison J (as he then was).

(2) Resolve inconsistencies between the Old Code and other legislation, such as the Land Registration Act 2002 and the Landlord and Tenant Act 1954;

(3) Clarify which third parties ought to be bound by rights conferred on telecoms network operators by landowners;

(4) Improve the procedure for resolving disputes arising under the Old Code;

(5) Clarify the process for terminating agreements falling under the Old Code; and

(6) Give limited new rights to telecoms network operators to upgrade and share their network equipment, given the emergence of new technologies that could enable telecoms network operators to save costs with the benefit of these new rights (passing those costs savings onto consumers).

In December 2014, HM Government's Department for Culture, Media and Sport (the Department for Digital, Culture, Media and Sport since 3 July 2017 – our emphasis) announced that it would reform the Old Code based on the Law Commission's recommendations. It consulted on its draft legislation between February and April 2015,[6] and published its revised proposals for a new code on 17 May 2016.[7]

HM Government's proposed reforms largely aligned with the Law Commission's original recommendations. This included the recommendation that any new code does not have retrospective effect, but instead provides for the Old Code to become 'naturally' obsolete as

---

[6] Department for Culture, Media and Sport, *Reforming the Electronic Communications Code: Consultation Document*, 26 February 2015.

[7] Department for Culture, Media and Sport, *A New Electronic Communications Code*, May 2016.

agreements subject to the Old Code are either terminated or renewed under the new regime.

However, following independent economic analysis, HM Government did decide to adopt a new (and controversial) basis for the valuation of rights conferred under agreements falling within the remit of the new statutory regime. Whereas the Old Code valued rights on an open market basis, the Code values them on a 'no scheme' basis, dramatically altering the potential value of the rights.

The result was the coming into force of the Code on 27 December 2017.

There have subsequently been substantial additions to the Code. The Telecommunications Infrastructure (Leasehold Property) Act 2021 ("**TILPA**") introduced a new Part 4A after Part 4 of Schedule 3A to the Communications Act 2003, to address the issue of unresponsive proposed grantors of agreements in relation to multiple dwelling buildings. Such applications are to be dealt with by the First-tier Tribunal. There have also been amendments to other parts of the Code by the Product Security and Telecommunications Infrastructure Act 2022 ("**PSTIA**"). Some parts of PSTIA are in force at the time of drafting. Other parts of PSTIA are not yet in force, but have been included in this book because it is anticipated that they will be in force soon. This includes the new Part 4ZA to the Code, to be added after Part 4 of the Code, which enables the Tribunal to impose agreements on non-responsive owners of relevant land in cases where the operator needs to install electronic communications equipment under or over relevant land, but does not need to install electronic communications equipment on the relevant land.

The Purpose of the Code

We have set out above that the Code is designed to regulate contractual relationships between telecoms network operators and landowners. But the Code itself does not clearly state why it exists; what purpose the regulation serves.

Assistance can instead be drawn from Law Commission's review of the Old Code. It says that a telecoms code needs to exist to (again, inexhaustibly):

(1) Ensure that the availability of telecoms services are not impeded by telecoms operators having difficulties gaining access to land;

(2) Strike a fair balance between the rights of landowners and the public interest in the provision of telecoms services across the United Kingdom; and

(3) Make certain the legal consequences of agreements between telecoms operators and landowners on third parties.[8]

In the following chapters, we will set out the various ways in which these envisioned purposes indeed ring true in the Code. In particular, the reader will see that the issue of whether a fair balance is struck between the public interest and the rights of landowners is central to both the extent of the court's power to impose code agreement terms on parties, and the new valuation basis for code agreements.

The Operation and Content of the Code and this Book

The Code creates a scheme whereby relevant telecoms operators can serve notice on landowners indicating a desire to acquire rights over their land for the purpose of furthering their telecoms networks. If the parties reach agreement on the terms of acquisition of those rights, then a qualifying agreement under the Code ("**code agreement**") is created. If the parties are in dispute, the courts will adjudicate (in an expedited timeframe) and impose a code agreement if relevant criteria are met.

---

[8] See Department for Culture, Media and Sport, *Reforming the Electronic Communications Code: Consultation Document*, 26 February 2015, Paragraphs 2.3 to 2.11 for a full digest of the Law Commission's views on the purpose of a telecoms code.

The core parts of the Code that are dealt with in this book are as follows:

(1) Part 1 of the Code, entitled 'Key Concepts',[9] sets out the various definitions that form the foundation for the Code. It deals with who the relevant telecoms operators are, what qualifies as telecoms apparatus and a telecoms network, and what core rights telecoms operators can seek to acquire under the Code ("**code rights**"). These matters are considered in more detail in Chapter Two;

(2) Part 2 of the Code, entitled 'Conferral of Code Rights and their Exercise',[10] is eclectic. It deals with the circumstances under which code rights can be exercised (Chapter Two), the relevant persons who can be compelled to enter into code agreements (Chapter Three), and the third parties that may be bound by code agreements (Chapters Three and Eleven);

(3) Part 3 of the Code, entitled 'Assignment of Code Rights, and Upgrading and Sharing of Apparatus',[11] is self-explanatory. The 'bonus rights' to upgrade and share telecoms apparatus are explored in Chapter Two, and assignment is considered in Chapter Eleven;

(4) Part 4 of the Code, entitled 'Power of the Court to Impose Agreement',[12] is far-reaching. It provides the power of the court to impose code agreement terms (Chapter Four), the formalities for code agreements and the kind of terms that can be included within code agreements (Chapter Five) and the new valuation basis (Chapter Seven);

(5) Part 4A of the Code, entitled 'Code rights in respect of land connected to leased premises: unresponsive occupiers',[13] together

---

[9]   Communications Act 2003, Schedule 3A, Paragraphs 1 to 7.

[10] Ibid, Paragraphs 8 to 14.

[11] Ibid, Paragraphs 15 to 18.

[12] Ibid, Paragraphs 19 to 27.

[13] Ibid, Paragraphs 27A to 27I.

with Part 4ZA of the Code (not yet In force), entitled 'Code rights In respect of land: unresponsive occupiers',[14] in Chapter 13. This considers the power of the First-tier Tribunal (Property Chamber) to impose agreements following a request by a leaseholder of a multiple dwelling building, in the case of Part 4A, and cases which involved installation of equipment under or over relevant land (but not on the relevant land), in the case of Part 4ZA (when Section 67 of PSTIA comes into force).

(6) Part 5 of the Code, entitled 'Termination and Modification of Agreements',[15] also contains the provisions for continuation and novation of code agreements. Continuation and termination are considered in Chapter Eight, whereas modification and novation are found in Chapter Nine;

(7) Part 6 of the Code, entitled 'Right to Require Removal of Electronic Communications Apparatus',[16] is dealt with in Chapter Ten; and

(8) In addition, this book contains chapters on landowners' rights to compensation payable under the Code (Chapter Seven), the transitional provisions bridging the Old Code and the Code (Chapter Twelve) and on alternative dispute resolution, and the procedures and practicalities of litigating under the Code (Chapter Fourteen).

This book does not pretend to comprehensively discuss every aspect of the Code. In particular, Parts 7 to 12 of the Code [17] lie outside the scope

---

[14] Ibid, Paragraphs 27ZB to 27ZI.

[15] Ibid, Paragraphs 28 to 35.

[16] Ibid, Paragraphs 36 to 44.

[17] Which deal with: conferral of transport land rights and their exercise; conferral of street work rights and their exercise; conferral of tidal water rights and their exercise; undertaker's works affecting electronic communications apparatus; overhead apparatus; and rights to object to certain apparatus installed on, over or under tidal water or lands.

of this book. As does detailed consideration of the workings of the Old Code.

Summary

In summary:

(1) The Code was not brought in simply because the Old Code was not up to the task of keeping up with developing technologies. The Old Code had a number of serious flaws, including poor drafting, and required extensive reform to operate satisfactorily both in the modern day and in the context of other statutory regimes;

(2) The Code regulates the contractual relationships between telecoms operators and landowners chiefly to ensure that the former has sufficient access to the land it needs to provide services that are in the public interest, and also to ensure that third parties can be certain where they stand in respect of those agreements;

(3) The Code operates by giving telecoms operators the power to compel landowners to enter into agreements with them for the conferral of code rights. Provided the relevant formalities are complied with, in default of agreement the courts will adjudicate the dispute and may impose a code agreement and decide its terms, including the payment of consideration and compensation. The Code also provides for the circumstances under which code agreements may be terminated (after which, when and how telecoms apparatus must be removed from the subject land) or varied; and

(4) New machinery under the Code now exists to empower the First-tier Tribunal to impose agreements following a request by a leaseholder of a multiple dwelling building, and in future it will be able to impose agreements in cases which involve installation of equipment under or over but not on relevant land, when Section 67 of PSTIA comes into force.

CHAPTER TWO

CODE OPERATORS, THEIR NETWORKS, AND CODE RIGHTS

This chapter explores the following:

(1) Which telecoms network operators are subject to the Code;

(2) What qualifies as telecoms apparatus and telecoms networks;

(3) The code rights and their exercise; and

(4) The power for telecoms network operators to upgrade or share their telecoms apparatus.

Code Operators

The Code is designed to regulate contractual relationships between landowners and certain telecoms network operators concerning rights granted in respect of telecoms apparatus. The relevant telecoms network operators are identified in Section 106 of the Communications Act 2003 ("**the 2003 Act**"):

"(3) The electronic communications code shall have effect—

(a) in the case of a person to whom it is applied by a direction given by OFCOM; and

(b) in the case of the Secretary of State or any Northern Ireland department where the Secretary of State or that department is providing or proposing to provide an electronic communications network.

THE ELECTRONIC COMMUNICATIONS CODE: A PRACTICAL GUIDE

(4) The only purposes for which the electronic communications code may be applied in a person's case by a direction under this section are—

(a) the purposes of the provision by him of an electronic communications network; or

(b) the purposes by him of a system of infrastructure which he is making available, or proposing to make available, for use by providers of electronic communications networks for the purposes of the provision by them of their networks.

(5) A direction applying the electronic communications code in any person's case may provide for that code to have effect in his case—

(a) in relation only to such places or localities as may be specified or described in the direction;

(b) for the purposes only of the provision of such electronic communications network, or part of an electronic communications network, as may be so specified or described; or

(c) for the purposes only of the provision of such system of infrastructure, or part of a system of infrastructure, as may be so specified or described." [1]

Pursuant to Section 108(1) of the 2003 Act, the Office of Communications ("**OFCOM**") keeps a register of all persons to whom the Code applies by virtue of a directive under Section 106.[2] At present, there are over 200 telecoms network operators on OFCOM's register ("**code operators**").

---

[1]   Communications Act 2003, Section 106(3) to (5).

[2]   The register can be found at https://www.ofcom.org.uk/phones-telecoms-and-internet/information-for-industry/policy/electronic-comm-code/register-of-persons-with-powers-under-the-electronic-communications-code.

Telecoms Apparatus and Networks

What qualifies as telecoms apparatus is set out in Paragraph 5 of the Code:

"(1) In this code "electronic communications apparatus" means—

(a) apparatus designed or adapted for use in connection with the provision of an electronic communications network,

(b) apparatus designed or adapted for a use which consists of or includes the sending or receiving of communications or other signals that are transmitted by means of an electronic communications network,

(c) lines, and

(d) other structures or things designed or adapted for use in connection with the provision of an electronic communications network…

(3) In this code—

"line" means any wire, cable, tube, pipe or similar thing (including its casing or coating) which is designed or adapted for use in connection with the provision of any electronic communications network or electronic communications service;

"structure" includes a building only if the sole purpose of that building is to enclose other electronic communications apparatus." [3]

The definition contains no reference to any specific type of equipment or to any kind of telecoms service that said equipment might facilitate. This wording was chosen carefully, upon a recommendation contained in the Law Commission's review of the Old Code, to ensure that the description of telecoms apparatus is 'technologically neutral'.[4] The goal

---

[3]   Communications Act 2003, Schedule 3A, Paragraph 5(1) and (3).

[4]   Department for Culture, Media and Sport, *Reforming the Electronic Communications Code: Consultation Document*, 26 February 2015, Paragraph 1.28.

being to ensure that, as telecoms technology evolves to the point that it no longer resembles existing technologies, the court does not find itself adjudicating disputes between telecoms operators and landowners about whether or not new telecoms equipment actually falls within the remit of the Code.

The definition of telecoms networks, contained in Paragraphs 6 and 7 of the Code, is given similar treatment, in order to have as broad a definition as possible. Paragraph 6 reads:

"In this code "network" in relation to an operator means—

(a) if the operator falls within paragraph 2(a), so much of any electronic communications network or infrastructure system provided by the operator as is not excluded from the application of the code under section 106(5), and

(b) if the operator falls within paragraph 2(b), the electronic communications network which the Secretary of State or the Northern Ireland department is providing or proposing to provide." [5]

And Paragraph 7 of the Code provides for a similarly wide definition of *"infrastructure system"*:

"(1) In this code "infrastructure system" means a system of infrastructure provided so as to be available for use by providers of electronic communications networks for the purposes of the provision by them of their networks.

(2) References in this code to provision of an infrastructure system include references to establishing or maintaining such a system."

---

[5] Communications Act 2003, Schedule 3A, Paragraph 6.

Code Rights and their Exercise

A Code right in respect of land may only be conferred on an operator by agreement between the occupier of the land and the operator in accordance with Paragraph 9(1) of the Code (as amended). However, where the operator has the right to share the use of electronic communications apparatus with another operator under or by an agreement under the Code, Paragraph 9(1) does not prevent the first operator from permitting the second operator to exercise the code right.[6]

Paragraph 3 of the Code as amended by Section 57 of the Product Security and Telecommunications Infrastructure Act 2022 ("**PSTIA**") with effect from 7 February 2023 sets out the twelve core rights that telecoms operators can seek to acquire from landowners under a code agreement:

"(1) For the purposes of this code a "code right", in relation to an operator and any land, is a right for the statutory purposes—

(a) to install electronic communications apparatus on, under or over the land,

(b) to keep installed electronic communications apparatus which is on, under or over the land,

(c) to inspect, maintain, adjust, alter, repair, upgrade or operate electronic communications apparatus which is on, under or over the land,

(ca) to share with another operator the use of electronic communications apparatus which the first operator keeps installed on, under or over the land,

---

6   Ibid, Paragraph 9(2).

(d) to carry out any works on the land for or in connection with the installation of electronic communications apparatus on, under or over the land or elsewhere,[7]

(e) to carry out any works on the land for or in connection with the maintenance, adjustment, alteration, repair, upgrading or operation of electronic communications apparatus which is on, under or over the land or elsewhere,

(ea) to carry out any works on the land for the purposes of, or in connection with, sharing with another operator the use of electronic communications apparatus which the first operator keeps installed on, under or over the land or elsewhere,

(f) to enter the land to inspect, maintain, adjust, alter, repair, upgrade or operate any electronic communications apparatus which is on, under or over the land or elsewhere,

(fa) to enter the land for the purposes of, or in connection with, sharing with another operator the use of electronic communications apparatus which the first operator keeps installed on, under or over the land or elsewhere,

(g) to connect to a power supply,

(h) to interfere with or obstruct a means of access to or from the land (whether or not any electronic communications apparatus is on, under or over the land), or

---

[7] In *EE Ltd v MacDonald* [2020] 3 WLUK 511 the Lands Tribunal (Scotland) held that Paragraph 3(d) of the Code should be interpreted widely enough (and purposively) so as to be capable of giving a code operator an express right to take access over land in order to install telecoms apparatus on other land. Whilst not binding in England and Wales, this decision remains informative.

(i) to lop or cut back, or require another person to lop or cut back, any tree or other vegetation that interferes or will or may interfere with electronic communications apparatus." [8]

By Paragraph 3(2) of the Code, references to "the first operator" in sub-paragraph (1) are to the operator mentioned in the opening words of that sub-paragraph.

And the definition of *"the statutory purposes"* is set out in Paragraph 4 of the Code:

"(a) in relation to sharing rights, the purposes of enabling the provision by other operators of their networks, and

(b) in relation to rights other than sharing rights—

> *(i) the purposes of providing the operator's network, or*

> *(ii) the purposes of providing an infrastructure system.*

(2) In sub-paragraph (1), "sharing right" means a right within paragraph 3(1)(ca), (ea) or (fa)." [9]

Most of these rights broadly mirror those that were available under the Old Code.[10] But some of the rights contained at Paragraph 3(1)(ca), (ea), (f), (fa), (g), (h) and (i) of the Code are either completely (or mostly) new:

(1) Under Paragraphs 3(1)(ca), (ea) and (fa) (each inserted by Section 57 of PSTIA) code operators can acquire rights to share their telecoms apparatus with other operators, carry out works to enable this, and enter land to facilitate this;

---

8   Ibid, Paragraph 3.

9   Ibid, Paragraph 4 as amended by Section57 of PSTIA.

10   See Telecommunications Act 1984, Schedule 2, Paragraph 2(1).

(2) Under Paragraph 3(1)(f) and (h), code operators can now acquire the right to access (or the right to obstruct access to) land neighbouring the land where they have installed their telecoms apparatus;

(3) Under Paragraph 3(1)(g), code operators can now acquire the right to connect their telecoms apparatus to a local power supply, paid for by the landowner. Any electricity used by the telecoms operator that is paid for by the landowner is likely to be reflected in the compensation payable by the telecoms operator to the landowner; and

(4) Under Paragraph 3(1)(i), what previously existed only as a power to give notice to an occupier of land to cut back a tree growing on their land has been turned into a code right that extends to all vegetation, not just to trees, [11] and allows the telecoms operator to choose between doing the work itself or requiring another to do it.[12]

Code rights, once acquired under a code agreement, can only be exercised in accordance with *"the terms subject to which it is conferred"* [13] and anything done by a code operator *"in the exercise of a code right conferred under this Part in relation to any land is to be treated as done in the exercise of a statutory power."* [14]

---

[11] Ibid, Paragraph 19.

[12] The old power to give notice to achieve similar as been retained and updated in Paragraph 82 of the Code. Under that provision, code operators may serve a notice on an occupier of land requiring them to lop back a tree or vegetation that may obstruct or interfere with their telecoms apparatus regardless of whether this has been conferred on the code operator by that person as a code right under a code agreement. There is then provision for a counter-notice to be served, and for the court to determine whether the code operator's notice takes effect (if not already complied with) and whether to award compensation. For notices generally, see Chapter Three.

[13] Communications Act 2003, Schedule 3A, Paragraph 12(1).

[14] Ibid, Paragraph 12(2).

The Power to Upgrade or Share Telecoms Apparatus

Also new are the two bonus rights to upgrade and share telecoms apparatus that are automatically conferred on all telecoms operators who enter into code agreements under Part 2 of the Code, which, unlike the sharing rights inserted at Paragraph 3(1)(ca), (ea) and (fa) by Section 57 of PSTIA, are automatically acquired together with any code rights set out at Paragraph 3(1).[15] These bonus rights are subject to two conditions, as set out in Paragraph 17 of the Code:

"(1) An operator ("the main operator") who has entered into an agreement under Part 2 of this code may, if the conditions in sub-paragraphs (2) and (3) are met—

(a) upgrade the electronic communications apparatus to which the agreement relates, or

(b) share the use of such electronic communications apparatus with another operator.

(2) The first condition is that any changes as a result of the upgrading or sharing to the electronic communications apparatus to which the agreement relates have no adverse impact, or no more than a minimal adverse impact, on its appearance.

(3) The second condition is that the upgrading or sharing imposes no additional burden on the other party to the agreement.

(4) For the purposes of sub-paragraph (3) an additional burden includes anything that—

---

[15] Save where the exercise of the code right conferred under the code agreement depends on a right that has effect pursuant to an agreement that was entered into under the Old Code. See Chapter Twelve and Digital Economy Act 2017, Schedule 2, Paragraph 5(2).

(a) has an additional adverse effect on the other party's enjoyment of the land, or

(b) causes additional loss, damage or expense to that party." [16]

Further, pursuant to Paragraph 17(5) of the Code, it is not possible to contract out of these bonus rights being conferred on the telecoms operator by the landowner. Nor is it possible to agree to make use of the 'bonus rights' subject to any conditions *"including a condition requiring the payment of money".*[17]

The interpretation of Paragraph 17 of the Code was one of the matters in dispute in <u>*On Tower UK Limited v JH & FW Green Limited*</u>.[18] The dispute included the extent of the disputed terms conferring rights to upgrade and share telecoms apparatus on a woodland site In the South Downs national park.

At first instance, the Tribunal broadly followed the approach it took in <u>*Cornerstone Telecommunications Infrastructure Ltd v London and Quadrant Housing Trust,*</u>[19] treating the bonus rights under Paragraph 17 as a floor, setting out the minimum rights a code operator is entitled to. This approach was approved by the Court of Appeal, who stressed that whereas the onus is on a code operator seeking more extensive rights than those conferred under Paragraph 17 of the Code to explain why it does so, the code operator does not need to establish *"pretty striking circumstances"* or *"pretty compelling circumstances"*, as advocated for by the respondent; instead, *"Each application must be assessed on Its particular merits."* [20]

---

16 Communications Act 2003, Schedule 3A, Paragraph 17(1) to (4).

17 Ibid, Paragraph 17(5).

18 [2022] 4 WLR 27.

19 [2020] UKUT 282 (LC). See in particular [73]-[77].

20 [2022] 4 WLR 27, [62]. The core reasoning at [61] being that, otherwise, the purpose of Paragraph 17 of the Code would be warped; it was not designed to

PSTIA Amendments in Force From 17 April 2023

Sections 58 and 59 of PSTIA are due to come into force on 17 April 2023.[21]

Section 58 amends Paragraph 5 of the Code in relation to code operators who are parties to subsisting agreements [22] and adds a new Paragraph 5A after Paragraph 5 to confer on these similar bonus upgrading and sharing rights as are conferred on code agreements imposed under the Code:

"5A Upgrading and sharing provisions

Paragraph 17 of the new code (power for operator to upgrade or share apparatus) applies in relation to an operator who is a party to a subsisting agreement, but as if for sub-paragraphs (1) to (6) there were substituted—

"(1) This paragraph applies where—

> *(a) an operator ("the main operator") keeps electronic communications apparatus installed under land, and*

> *(b) the main operator is a party to a subsisting agreement in relation to the electronic communications apparatus.*

(2) If the conditions in sub-paragraphs (3), (4) and (6) are met, the main operator may—

> *(a) upgrade the electronic communications apparatus, or*

> *(b) share the use of the electronic communications apparatus with another operator.*

---

provide a barrier to acquiring upgrading and sharing rights beyond those given automatically, but to give some such rights without any need for argument.

[21] Pursuant to Product Security and Telecommunications Infrastructure Act 2022 (Commencement No.1) Regulations (SI 2023/109).

[22] For which, see Chapter Twelve.

(3) The first condition is that the upgrading or sharing has no adverse impact on the land.

(4) The second condition is that the upgrading or sharing imposes no burden on any person with an interest in the land.

(5) For the purposes of sub-paragraph (4) a burden includes anything that—

> *(a) has an adverse effect on the person's enjoyment of the land, or*

> *(b) causes loss, damage or expense to the person.*

(6) The third condition is that, before the beginning of the period of 21 days ending with the day on which the main operator begins to upgrade the electronic communications apparatus or (as the case may be) share its use, the main operator attaches a notice, in a secure and durable manner, to a conspicuous object on the relevant land."

Further, Paragraph 5A(11) reads:

"(11) References in this paragraph to sharing electronic communications apparatus include carrying out works to the electronic communications apparatus to enable such sharing to take place."

And Paragraph 5A(12) clarifies that:

"(12) In this paragraph—

"the relevant land" means—

(a) in a case where the main operator has a right to enter the land under which the electronic communications apparatus is installed, that land;

> *(b) in any other case, the land on which works will be carried out to enable the upgrading or sharing to take place or, where there is more than one set of works, the land on which each set of works will be carried out;*

"subsisting agreement" has the meaning given by paragraph 1(4) of Schedule 2 to the Digital Economy Act 2017."

Save for the notice condition at the new Paragraph 5A(6), the bonus rights conferred under Paragraph 5A substantially mirror those given under Paragraph 17. At Paragraph 5A(7), the requirements for such notices [23] are set out:

"(7) A notice attached for the purposes of sub-paragraph (6) must—

(a) be attached in a position where it is reasonably legible,

(b) state that the main operator intends to upgrade the electronic communications apparatus or (as the case may be) share its use with another operator,

(c) state the date on which the main operator intends to begin to upgrade the electronic communications apparatus or (as the case may be) share its use with another operator,

(d) state, in a case where the main operator intends to share the use of the electronic communications apparatus with another operator, the name of the other operator, and

(e) give the name of the main operator and an address in the United Kingdom at which the main operator may be contacted about the upgrading or sharing." [24]

Just as under Paragraph 17(5) of the Code, Paragraph 5A(9) renders agreements contracting out of these bonus rights void.

Paragraph 5A(10) then provides that these bonus rights are not to be read as automatically conferring code rights to share (i.e. those new

---

[23] For notices generally, see Chapter Three.

[24] The address given pursuant to Paragraph 5A(7)(e) counts as being given pursuant to Paragraph 91(2) of the Code, per Paragraph 5A(8). The relevance of this is address in Chapter Three.

code rights inserted at Paragraph 3(1)(ca), (ea) and (fa) of the Code by Section 57 of PSTIA).

Section 59 of PSTIA then extends very similar rights to telecoms apparatus installed under land prior to 29 December 2003, by insertion of a new Paragraph 17A after Paragraph 17 of the Code.

Paragraph 17A substantially mirrors the new Paragraph 5. Its core difference is that Is applies only to telecoms apparatus installed *"under land… before 29 December 2003"*, and In respect of this the code operator Is not party to an agreement under Part 2 of the Code.

Summary

In summary:

(1) The Code only applies to those telecoms operators who have received a directive from OFCOM, and are contained in OFCOM's official register (and Secretaries of State);

(2) Both telecoms equipment and telecoms networks have been 'technologically neutral' definitions to future-proof the Code against the development of new telecoms technologies and systems;

(3) We have set out the code rights themselves, and how they broadly mirror the rights under the Old Code save for new rights to connect to a power supply, access and obstruct access to neighbouring land, and lop or cut back any vegetation that may interfere with telecoms equipment; and

(4) Bonus rights to share and upgrade telecoms apparatus are conferred automatically with all code agreements, but these rights are an *"irreducible minimum"* that can only be exercised if two conditions are met. It is possible for code operators to seek code rights to upgrade and share that go beyond those conditions, and whether such terms are to be included will be determined on its own merits as with other discretionary terms. These rights are extended with effect from 17

April 2023 to subsisting agreements and apparatus installed under land prior to 29 December 2003, subject to additional notice constraints.

CHAPTER THREE

NOTICES, THEIR SERVICE, AND PARAGRAPH 20 NOTICES

This chapter deals with the following topics:

(1) The general requirements for all forms of notice given under the Code;

(2) Service of notices given under the Code;

(3) How code operators commence the process of entering code agreements by serving a notice pursuant to Paragraph 20 of the Code ("**Paragraph 20 notice**"); and

(4) The identity of the *"relevant person"* upon whom the Paragraph 20 notice should be served.

The General Requirements for Notices Given Under the Code

Part 15 of the Code contains the provisions in respect of notices given under the Code generally.

Notices Given by Code Operators

Paragraph 88 of the Code sets out the requirements for all notices given by code operators. Such notices must:

"(a) explain the effect of the notice,

(b) explain which provisions of this code are relevant to the notice, and

(c) explain the steps that may be taken by the recipient in respect of the notice."[1]

As set out above, OFCOM are obliged by Paragraph 90(1) of the Code to prescribe all forms of notice that can be given under the Code, and have done so. OFCOM's prescribed form of notices must be used by code operators.[2]

Failure to comply with the requirements of Paragraph 88 of the Code renders any notice given by a code operator invalid,[3] unless the person receiving the notice chooses to rely on the notice and treat it as valid.[4]

Notices Given by Others

Pursuant to Paragraphs 89(1) to (4) of the Code:

(1) OFCOM's prescribed form of notice to be given under Paragraphs 31(1) (termination notices)[5] 33(1) (variation notices),[6] 39(1) and 40(2) (notices relating to the identification and removal of telecoms apparatus)[7] of the Code must be used by persons other than code operators;[8] and

---

[1]   Communications Act 2003, Schedule 3A, Paragraph 88(1).

[2]   Ibid, Paragraph 88(2). And a certificate issued by OFCOM stating that a particular form of notice used by a code operator has been prescribed by them is conclusive evidence of that fact, pursuant to Paragraph 88(5).

[3]   Ibid, Paragraph 88(3).

[4]   Ibid, Paragraph 88(4).

[5]   For which, see Chapter Eight.

[6]   For which, see Chapter Nine.

[7]   For which, see Chapter Ten.

[8]   Communications Act 2003, Schedule 3A, Paragraphs 89(1) and (2). And a certificate issued by OFCOM stating that a particular form of notice used by a person other than a code operator has been prescribed by them is conclusive evidence of that fact, pursuant to Paragraph 89(7).

(2) Failure to do so renders any notice given invalid, unless the code operator chooses to rely upon the notice received and treat it as valid.[9]

Where:

(1) A notice is given by a code operator to an other person ("**the Operator's Notice**"),

(2) The other person gives a notice in response to the Operator's Notice ("**the Responding Notice**") (e.g. a relevant counter-notice),

(3) OFCOM have prescribed the form of Responding Notice, and

(4) The operator, when giving the Operator's Notice, drew the other person's attention to the prescribed form of Responding Notice – [10]

the Operator's Notice is a valid notice for the purposes of the Code regardless, but if the other person has failed to use the form prescribed by OFCOM then *"the person giving the notice must bear any costs incurred by the operator as a result of the notice not being in that form"*.[11]

It follows that where the code operator fails, when giving the Operator's Notice, to draw the other person's attention to the prescribed form of Responding Notice then a failure to use that prescribed form by the other person:

(1) Does not render the Responding Notice invalid; and

(2) The other person will not be liable to bear the code operator's costs incurred as a result of the Responding Notice not being in the prescribed form.

---

[9] Ibid, Paragraphs 89(3) and (4).

[10] Communications Act 2003, Schedule 3A, Paragraph 89(5).

[11] Ibid, Paragraph 89(6).

The Service of Notices Given Under the Code

Service of notices given under the Code is dealt with at Paragraph 91:

"(1) A notice given under this code must not be sent by post unless it is sent by a registered post service or by recorded delivery.

(2) For the purposes, in the case of a notice under this code, of section 394 of this Act (service of notifications and other documents) and section 7 of the Interpretation Act 1978 (references to service by post), the proper address of a person ("P") is–

(a) if P has given the person giving the notice an address for service under this code that address, and

(b) otherwise, the address given by section 394." [12]

Section 394 of the 2003 Act sets out that notices required to be sent under the Code may be delivered to the relevant person, left at their *"proper address"* or be sent by post to their *"proper address"*.[13] Further, that:

"(4) The notification or document may be given or sent to a body corporate by being given or sent to the secretary or clerk of that body.

(5) The notification or document may be given or sent to a firm by being given or sent to–

(a) a partner in the firm; or

(b) a person having the control or management of the partnership business."

---

[12] Ibid, Paragraph 91(1) and (2).

[13] Communications Act 2003, Section 394(3).

(6) The notification or document may be given or sent to an unincorporated body or association by being given or sent to a member of the governing body of the body or association.

(7) For the purposes of this section and section 7 of the Interpretation Act 1978 (c. 30) (service of documents by post) in its application to this section, the proper address of that person is–

(a) in the case of body corporate, the address of the registered or principal office of the body;

(b) in the case of a firm, unincorporated body or association, the address of the principal office of the partnership, body or association;

(c) in the case of a person to whom the notification or other document is given or sent in reliance on any of subsections (4) to (6), the proper address of the body corporate, firm or (as the case may be) other body or association in question; and

(d) in any other case, the last known address of the person in question." [14]

And for companies registered outside the United Kingdom, firms carrying on business outside the United Kingdom, or unincorporated bodies or associations with offices outside the United Kingdom, references in Section 394(7) of the 2003 Act to *"its principal office includes references to its principal office within the United Kingdom (if any)."* [15]

Section 394 of the 2003 Act is expressly subject to Section 395, which provides for service by electronic means making use of a telecoms network.[16] Section 395 of the 2003 Act provides that (for example) e-mail service of a notice *"has effect for the purposes of the enactments specified in section 394(2) as a delivery of the notification or other document to the*

---

[14] Ibid, Section 394(4) to (7).

[15] Ibid, Section 394(8).

[16] Ibid, Section 394(10).

recipient, but only if the requirements imposed by or under this section are complied with." [17]

There are then different requirements depending on whom the notice is to be served. Provided that the intended recipient is not OFCOM itself, the recipient (or any agent of the recipient) *"must have indicated to the person making the transmission the recipient's willingness to receive notifications or documents transmitted in the form and manner used."* [18] Such an indication:

"(a) must be given to [the person making the transmission] *in such manner as he may require;*

(b) may be a general indication or one that is limited to notifications or documents of a particular description;

(c) must state the address to be used and must be accompanied by such other information as that person requires for the making of the transmission; and

(d) may be modified or withdrawn at any time by a notice given to that person in such manner as he may require." [19]

So, notices given under the Code can be delivered to the recipient, delivered to their *"proper address"*, or posted to them at their *"proper address"* (provided that the notice is sent by registered post or recorded delivery). Provided that willingness to receive a notice by electronic means has been given by the recipient to the transmitter, service by (for example) e-mail is permitted and takes effect as a delivery to the recipient.

Paragraph 91 goes on, however, to explain how service of a relevant notice may be effected in the event that it is not possible to find out after *"reasonable enquiries the name and address of a person who is"* either the

---

[17]   Ibid, Section 395(2).

[18]   Ibid, Section 395(5). For notices served on OFCOM, see Section 395(3) and (4).

[19]   Ibid, Section 395(6).

"occupier of land for the purposes of this code" or *"the owner of an interest in land."* [20] In respect of the former –

"(4) A notice may be given under this code to the occupier —

(a) by addressing it to a person by the description of "occupier" of the land (and describing the land), and

(b) by delivering it to a person who is on the land or, if there is no person on the land to whom it can be delivered, by affixing it, or a copy of it, to a conspicuous object on the land" [21] –

and of the latter –

"(6) A notice may be given under this code to the owner—

(a) by addressing it to a person by the description of "owner" of the interest (and describing the interest and the land), and

(b) by delivering it to a person who is on the land or, if there is no person on the land to whom it can be delivered, by affixing it, or a copy of it, to a conspicuous object on the land." [22]

Paragraph 20 Notices

One of the most important notices that can be given under the Code is the Paragraph 20 notice, which is given by a code operator when it has identified a piece of land over which it has decided to acquire one or more code rights in order to improve its telecoms network. Rather than simply approaching the landowner and seeking to negotiate terms, the code operator must serve a Paragraph 20 notice. Paragraph 20 of the Code provides that:

---

[20]   Ibid, Schedule 3A, Paragraph 91(3) and (5).

[21]   Ibid, Paragraph 91(4).

[22]   Ibid, Paragraph 91(6).

"(1) ... where the operator requires a person (a "relevant person") to agree—

(a) to confer a code right on the operator, or

(b) to be otherwise bound by a code right which is exercisable by the operator.

(2) The operator may give the relevant person a notice in writing—

(a) setting out the code right, and all of the other terms of the agreement that the operator seeks, and

(b) stating that the operator seeks the person's agreement to those terms." [23]

Pursuant to Paragraph 90 of the Code, OFCOM must prescribe *"the form of a notice to be given under each provision of this code that requires a notice to be given."* [24] The template notices prescribed by OFCOM, including its template Paragraph 20 notice, can be found hosted on its website.[25]

But Paragraph 20 of the Code alone, which provides for the service of a Paragraph 20 notice as a prerequisite to the acquisition of permanent code rights (after agreement has been reached with the relevant person, or a determination has been made by the Court), does not set out all the circumstances in which code operators may wish to serve a Paragraph 20 Notice.

Indeed, Paragraph 26(3) of the Code provides that *"if (and only if) the operator has given the* [relevant person] *a notice which complies with paragraph 20(2) stating that an agreement is sought on an interim basis..."* it is possible for the code operator to seek that the court grant the code

---

[23] Communications Act 2003, Schedule 3A, Paragraph 20(1) and (2).

[24] Ibid, Paragraph 90(1).

[25] Before prescribing these notices, OFCOM was obliged to consult with code operators *"and such other persons as OFCOM think appropriate"* pursuant to Paragraph 90(3) of the Code.

operator code rights on an interim basis pending final determination (or agreement) of the terms of the code agreement.[26]

Further, Paragraph 27 of the Code provides that a Paragraph 20 notice can seek that the relevant person agree to confer code rights to a code operator on a temporary basis.[27] But this provision only applies in circumstances where telecoms apparatus is already installed on the land in question.

Importantly, it appears that the court has no power to impose code rights in a code agreement that are not expressly sought in a valid Paragraph 20 notice. This was explained by Martin Rodger QC at [88] of his judgment in _Cornerstone Telecommunications Infrastructure Ltd v Compton Beauchamp Estates Ltd_:

"Paragraph 20 of the Code lays down a procedure for the imposition of Code rights which the Tribunal is not free to depart from. That procedure requires the operator to identify in its notice under paragraph 20(2) inviting agreement [to] _both the Code right and "all of the other terms of the agreement that the operator seeks"… it is those rights, and no more, which the operator may apply to the Tribunal to have imposed on the unwilling occupier of the land (we say nothing at this stage about whether an application can be made for lesser rights)."_ [28]

---

[26] Communications Act 2003, Schedule 3A, Paragraph 26(3). In _EE Ltd v MacDonald_ [2020] 3 WLUK 511 the Lands Tribunal (Scotland) held that a Paragraph 20 notice seeking interim code rights does not have to specify the length of the term of the code agreement sought, as this requirement does not apply to notices, only under Paragraph 11 of the Code to code agreements (for which, see Chapter Five). This decision, albeit not binding in England and Wales, would be of general application to Paragraph 20 notices seeking code rights, interim code rights and temporary code rights.

[27] Ibid, Paragraph 27(1).

[28] [2019] UKUT 107 (LC). This was the first instance decision in _Compton Beauchamp_. This element of the Deputy President's judgment was not appealed, and so was not subsequently reconsidered by the Court of Appeal.

The note in parentheses should not be ignored: there is, as of yet, no authority on whether, after having served a Paragraph 20 notice, the code operator can ask the court to impose lesser rights (or rights on different terms) to what was proposed in the notice. However, we anticipate that the court will be reluctant to make such an order. The court will more likely adopt the approach taken in *EE Ltd and Hutchison 3G UK Ltd v Stephenson and AP Wireless II (UK) Ltd*,[29] where it was held that a code operator seeking to vary a code agreement is not entitled to apply for variation on terms different to what were contained in its variation notice given under Paragraph 33 of the Code.[30]

How applications for code rights, interim code rights and temporary code rights progress after the service of a valid Paragraph 20 notice is covered in Chapter Four.

It should be noted that under Section 69 of the Product Security and Telecommunications Infrastructure Act 2022 ("**PSTIA**") (which is not yet in force at the time of publication) makes an amendment to Paragraph 20 of the Code,[31] which requires a Paragraph 20 notice to contain information about ADR and the consequences of refusing to engage in ADR. Further, the operator is to be required to consider ADR if it is reasonably practicable to do so before making an application by a new Sub-paragraph (5), and providing at Sub-paragraph (6) for notice to be given by either the operator or the relevant person that they wish to engage in ADR.

It should be noted that Section 69(5) of PSTIA will insert into Paragraph 96 of the Code power for the Tribunal to make awards of costs on the basis of *"any unreasonable refusal by a party to engage in alternative dispute resolution."*

---

[29] [2021] UKUT 167 I.

[30] For which, see Chapter Nine.

[31] To be inserted at a new Paragraph 20(2A).

The Relevant Person Under Paragraph 20

There are two classes of relevant person under Paragraph 20 of the Code, as identified by the two kinds of applications that can be made under Paragraph 20(1):

(1) Those who can be compelled to confer a code right on the code operator, pursuant to Paragraph 20(1)(a); and

(2) Those who can be compelled to be bound by a code right already conferred on a code operator by another, pursuant to Paragraph 20(1)(b).

<u>The Relevant Person under Paragraph 20(1)(a)</u>

The identity of this person was the core issue in dispute in the three separate appeals heard simultaneously in *Cornerstone Telecommunications Infrastructure Ltd v Compton Beauchamp Estates Ltd*;[32] the first matters under the Code to be considered by the Supreme Court.

For the purposes of this section, it is useful to understand the facts of the first appeal, which gives the case its name.[33] They are (n summary):

(1) The landowner, Compton Beauchamp Estates Ltd ("**Compton**"), granted Vodafone a lease of land with rights of access in 2004, upon which Vodafone built a telecoms mast;

(2) The lease expired in 2014, and Vodafone thereafter continued to occupy the site under a tenancy (the species of which was also in dispute between Compton and Vodafone);

---

[32] [2022] UKSC 18; [2022] 1 WLR 3360.

[33] The second appeal, being an appeal from the Court of Appeal in *Cornerstone Telecommunications Infrastructure Ltd v Ashloch Ltd* [2021] EWCA Civ 90, is considered in more detail in Chapter Twelve. The third appeal, which 'leapfrogged' from the Upper Tribunal in *Arqiva Services Ltd v AP Wireless II (UK) Ltd* [2020] UKUT 195 (LC), is also covered in Chapter Twelve.

(3) From August 2014, Vodafone had been sharing use of the telecoms mast with Telefonica;

(4) Cornerstone Telecommunications Infrastructure Ltd ("**Cornerstone**") was created as a joint venture by Vodafone and Telefonica, to own and manage a portfolio of telecoms sites contributed to by both. Cornerstone subsequently became a code operator under the Code

(5) In October 2017, Compton gave Vodafone notice to determine a tenancy at will, and sought possession of the land. Vodafone defended on the basis that it had a periodic tenancy;

(6) Cornerstone gave Compton a Paragraph 20 notice in December 2017 (practically as soon as the Code came into force), whilst Vodafone remained in occupation of the site; and

(7) Compton refused to grant Cornerstone any code rights, or to enter into any code agreement with it, on the basis that Vodafone and not Compton was the relevant person under Paragraph 20.

Lady Rose JSC, who gave the unanimous judgment of the Supreme Court, ultimately agreed with Compton. She began from the starting point that the word 'occupier' *"when It appears in different statutory provisions has no fixed meaning but must take its content from the context in which it appears and the purpose of the provisions in which it is used."*[34] The correct approach was therefore *"to work out how the regime Is Intended to work and the consider what meaning should be given to the word "occupier" so as to best achieve that goal."*[35]

The Supreme Court held that it is inherent in Paragraph 9 of the Code that the "operator" who seeks a code right must be different from the

---

[34] [2022] UKSC 18; [2022] 1 WLR 3360, [102].

[35] Ibid, [106].

"occupier of the land" also referred to therein.[36] Paragraph 9 of the Code reads:

"A code right in respect of land may only be conferred on an operator by an agreement between the occupier of the land and the operator."

Lady Rose JSC goes to explain that *"where an operator requests or applies for code rights under paragraph 20 of the new Code, it is not to be regarded as the occupier of the site for the purposes of paragraph 9 merely because it has* [telecoms apparatus] *installed on that site because of code rights that have previously been conferred on it for that equipment on that site. To hold otherwise would be to frustrate the way the Code should operate."* [37]

This led the Supreme Court to the following vital conclusion:

"The proper implementation of the Code does not require that all occupation of any operator with [telecoms apparatus] *installed on the site falls to be disregarded. The interpretation of paragraph 9 set out above means only that it is the occupation (if any) of the operator who seeks to have a new code right conferred on it which is ignored when considering how to identify the "occupier of the land" ... If, having allowed for this, it can be seen that another person who happens to be an operator is "the occupier of the land for the time being" (paragraph 105(1)), then the operator seeking to have the new code right has to approach that person (and any person who would also need to be bound) to seek their agreement."* [38]

It is for this reason that Cornerstone's reference failed. If Vodafone, who on the facts was the occupier of the land, had applied for new code rights then its own occupation would have been ignored when determining the Identity of the occupier for the purposes of a Paragraph 20 Notice,

---

[36] Ibid, [116].

[37] Ibid, [137]. The detailed discussion of the policy reasons behind the Supreme Court's reasoning as to how the Code should operate are set out at [118]-[136], and are worth reading in full in order to acquire a better holistic understanding of (in particular) the interrelationship between Parts 2 and 5 of the Code, the latter of which is the subject of Chapter Eight.

[38] Ibid, [140].

making Compton the proper recipient. But because it was Cornerstone who was seeking the code rights Vodafone's occupation was not to be ignored, Cornerstone should have served Vodafone with the notice, not Compton.[39]

It Is worth noting that the Supreme Court also undertook a textual analysis of the Code, and found that their above analysis was consistent with the Code's other provisions, including:

(1) How Paragraph 26 envisages a code operator with interim code rights [40] who has Installed equipment on the site and thereby taken occupation can make an application for full rights under Paragraph 20;[41]

(2) That the same is even more clearly the case where temporary rights [42] are conferred under Paragraph 27 because such rights can only be applied for where telecoms apparatus is already installed on, under or over the land;[43]

(3) How Paragraph 40(8) of the Code provides that the Tribunal cannot make an order for the removal of apparatus [44] from the site If an application under Paragraph 20 has been made and has not yet been resolved;[45]

(4) How otherwise, the transitional provisions between the Old Code and the Code would *"operate so randomly to the potentially great*

---

[39] See ibid, [162]-[164].

[40] For which, see Chapter Four.

[41] [2022] UKSC 18; [2022] 1 WLR 3360, [144].

[42] For which, see Chapter Four.

[43] [2022] UKSC 18; [2022] 1 WLR 3360, [145].

[44] For which, see Chapter Ten.

[45] [2022] UKSC 18; [2022] 1 WLR 3360, [150].

detriment of an operator in Vodafone's position as at 28 December 2017";[46] and

(5) How otherwise, the legislation carefully crafted to ensure that there is no real overlap between the Code and protections afforded under Part II of the Landlord and Tenant Act 1954 [47] may instead result in a lacuna in niche circumstances.[48]

<u>The Relevant Person under Paragraph 20(1)(b)</u>

The relevant person under Paragraph 20(1)(b) of the Code can be identified by reading Paragraph 20(1) – *"This paragraph applies where the operator requires a person (a "relevant person") to agree– …*

(b) to be otherwise bound by a code right which is exercisable by the operator." –

together with Paragraph 10(4) of the Code:

"The code right also binds any other person with an interest in the land who has agreed to be bound by it."

When these provisions are read together, it becomes clear that the relevant person under Paragraph 20(1)(b) of the Code is *"any other person with an interest in the land"*, where the said land is already subject to *"a code right which is exercisable by the operator"*.

Summary

In summary:

(1) Notices given by code operators must be in a prescribed form (unless relied upon by the recipient in any event), and sufficiently explain

---

[46] Ibid, [155]. Lady Rose JSC's reasoning is at [151]-[154].

[47] For which, see Chapters Eight and Thirteen.

[48] [2022] UKSC 18; [2022] 1 WLR 3360, [157].

themselves in order to be valid. Notices given by other persons must be in a prescribed form (unless relied upon by the recipient in any event), with the exception of notices given in response to notices from code operators – those notices are valid even if the prescribed form is not used, but the other person sending the notice may be liable for the code operator's costs incurred as a result of failure to comply if the code operator made the other person aware of the prescribed form of notice;

(2) There is a detailed scheme for service of notices under the Code. Delivery by hand to the relevant person, by hand to their proper address, or by post (recorded or special delivery only) are valid, and service by electronic means can become valid with appropriate consent. Where the identity of the relevant person cannot be found, the notice can be served to any person on the land over which the telecoms operator wishes to acquire code rights, or by affixing it to the said land;

(3) Telecoms operators begin the process of entering code agreements by serving a Paragraph 20 notice on the relevant person. The notice needs to be in the form prescribed by OFCOM, and telecoms operators cannot seek rights in excess of what is contained in their Paragraph 20 notice;

(4) The relevant person under Paragraph 21(1)(a) of the Code is the occupier of the land for the time being, ignoring the code operator itself if it would otherwise be the occupier; and

(5) The relevant person under Paragraph 21(1)(b) of the Code is any other person with an interest in land, where that land is already subject to a code right exercisable by the code operator.

CHAPTER FOUR

THE IDENTITY OF "THE COURT", AND APPLICATIONS TO IT TO ACQUIRE CODE RIGHTS

This chapter outlines:

(1) The identity of *"the court"*;

(2) The applications that can be made by code operators to *"the court"* for it to impose code rights, interim code rights and temporary code rights on relevant persons in the absence of agreement following service of a valid Paragraph 20 notice;

(3) What test should be applied by *"the court"* when determining whether to impose code rights; and

(4) The redevelopment defence available to relevant persons who want to avoid having a code right imposed on them.

The Upper Tribunal is Usually *"the court"*

Although the Code uses the term *"the court"* throughout,[1] the bodies who will in practice exercise the jurisdiction of *"the court"* are set out in

---

[1] Which pursuant to Paragraphs 94(1) and (2) of Schedule 3A to the Communications Act 2003 refers to *"in relation to England and Wales the county court"* subject to any regulations made under Paragraph 95.

Regulation 3 of the Electronic Communications Code (Jurisdiction) Regulations 2017("**the 2017 Regulations**")[2] as follows: [3]

"(1)... (aa)   in relation to England and Wales, the First-tier Tribunal and the Upper Tribunal, and

(c)   In relation to Scotland, the Lands Tribunal for Scotland...

(2)   Functions are exercisable by the First-tier Tribunal under paragraph 1(aa) only -

(a)   in connection with relevant proceedings In relation to England that have been transferred to the First-tier Tribunal by the Upper Tribunal, and

(b)   in connection with Part 4A proceedings (whether in relation to England and Wales).

Regulation 4 then goes on to provide that relevant proceedings must be commenced in the Upper Tribunal in England and Wales, or in the Lands Tribunal in Scotland, unless they are brought under Part 4A of the Code, in which case they must be commenced in the First-tier Tribunal In England and Wales, or in the sheriff court In Scotland.

Further, the Upper Tribunal ("**the Tribunal**") has the power to transfer cases to the First-tier Tribunal where appropriate under Rule 5(k) of the Tribunal Procedure (Upper Tribunal) (Lands Chamber) Rules 2010 as amended [4] ("**the Rules**").

It follows then that, save for applications under Part 4A or made elsewhere under the Code that are transferred down to the First-tier Tribunal by the Upper Tribunal applications , *"the court"* will be the Upper Tribunal.

---

[2]   SI 2017/1284.

[3]   Pursuant to Paragraph 95 of the Code.

[4]   And now in consolidated form, which has been in effect since 21 July 2020.

On 26 January 2018, The Honourable Mr Justice Holgate issued the Practice Note: Electronic Communications Code ("**the Practice Note**") (not a formal Practice Direction). At Paragraph 10 of the Practice Note, His Lordship noted that "...*For the time being it is not anticipated that Code disputes would normally be transferred by the Tribunal to the First-tier Tribunal, but parties who agree that their dispute should be determined in the First-tier Tribunal may apply for transfer to be considered.*"

The Practice Note recorded that proceedings which may be issued only in the Tribunal are proceedings under the following provisions of the Code:

"*Part 4 (Power of the court to impose agreement)*

Part 5 (Termination and modification of agreements)

Part 6 (Removal of Electronic Communications Apparatus)

Para. 53 (Alternation of apparatus at request of transport undertakers)

Part 12 (Rights to object to certain apparatus)

Part 13 (Right to lop trees)."[5]

Whereas the Tribunal does have the power to transfer relevant proceedings to the county court, should it consider the county court to be the more appropriate forum for the determination of those proceedings,[6] in practice "*the court*" will almost always be the Tribunal. At the time of writing, we are not aware of any case in which the Tribunal

---

[5]   The Practice Note accords entirely with Regulation 2 and 4(a) of the 2017 Regulations, the latter of which provides that proceedings under all of these parts of the Code "*must be commenced– (a) in relation to England and Wales, in the Upper Tribunal*".

[6]   Regulation 5 of the 2017 Regulations.

have opted to transfer any part of a relevant application to the county court.[7]

Applications Under Paragraph 20 of the Code: Code Rights

The requirements for a valid Paragraph 20 notice are set out in Chapter Three.

Following the service of a valid Paragraph 20 notice, pursuant to Paragraphs 20(3) and (4) of the Code, a code operator:

"(3) ... may apply to the court for an order under this paragraph if–

(a) the relevant person does not, before the end of 28 days beginning with the day on which the notice is given, agree to confer or be otherwise bound by the code right, or

(b) at any time after the notice is given, the relevant person gives notice in writing to the operator that the person does not agree to confer or otherwise be bound by the code right.

(4) An order under this paragraph is one which imposes on the operator and the relevant person an agreement between them which–

(a) confers the code right on the operator, or

(b) provides for the code right to bind the relevant person."[8]

So, if the code operator and the relevant person (identified in Chapter Three) are able to agree terms within the twenty-eight-day period after the service of the Paragraph 20 notice, no application under Paragraph 20 of the Code need be made. If this is not possible, then the code operator only acquires the ability to apply to the Tribunal after the

---

7   And the Practice Note does not shed any light on when the Upper Tribunal may consider doing so.

8   Communications Act 2003, Schedule 3A, Paragraphs 20(3) and (4).

twenty-eight-day period has expired, or after receiving notice in writing from the relevant person confirming that no agreement will be reached.

Code agreements imposed by order under Paragraph 20 of the Code take effect as an agreement under Part 2.[9]

Applications Under Paragraph 26 of the Code: Interim Code Rights

Similarly, Paragraphs 26 of the Code provides that a code operator may apply to the Tribunal for an order imposing the conferral of interim code rights.[10] Under Paragraph 26(2), an order can provide for the code operator and relevant person to be bound by the agreement:

"(a) for the period specified in the order, or

(b) until the occurrence of an event specified in the order."[11]

Just as with an application under Paragraph 20, the Tribunal an only make an order under Paragraph 26 if the code operator has given the relevant person a Paragraph 20 notice stating that a code agreement is sought on an interim basis.[12] Further, Paragraphs 22 to 25 and 84 of the Code (which provide for the effect of a code agreement, the terms that can be imposed on parties by the Tribunal, and the payment of consideration and compensation) all apply in applications under Paragraph 26 just as they do to applications under Paragraph 20.[13]

---

[9] Ibid, Paragraph 22.

[10] Ibid, Paragraph 26(1).

[11] Ibid, Paragraph 26(2).

[12] Ibid, Paragraph 26(3).

[13] Ibid, Paragraph 26(4). Although it was held by the Lands Tribunal (Scotland) in *British Telecommunications Plc v Morrison* [2020] 8 WLUK 259 at [4] that *"whatever the position may be for applications for full code rights"* the notice relied on in an application for interim code rights is not required to state a term as to the payment of consideration. This decision was premised on the effect of Paragraph 26(6)(b), which provides that *"the duty in paragraph 23 to include terms as to the*

Unlike applications under Paragraph 20, the code operator can apply to the Tribunal immediately after giving the Paragraph 20 notice, and may make an order conferring interim code rights *"if the court thinks the order should be made as a matter of urgency."* [14] Also, from the time that the period specified in the order expires, or the event specified in the order takes place, the relevant person:

"has the right, subject to and in accordance with Part 6 of this code, to require the operator to remove any electronic communications apparatus placed on the land under the agreement imposed under this paragraph." [15]

So whilst interim code rights can be applied for under similar circumstances to 'standard' Paragraph 20 applications, they can be applied for earlier,[16] and terminate without the need for further action at the time provided for by the Tribunal.[17] It should be noted, however, that it is not open to parties to enter into an agreement for interim code rights by consent.[18]

Further, the Court of Appeal have ruled that there is no requirement for an application under Paragraph 26 to be accompanied by an application under Paragraph 20: an application for interim code rights can stand on

---

payment of consideration to that person in an agreement [applies to Paragraph 26 as if it] *were a power to do so."* Given this decision is not binding in England and Wales, best practice is still likely to specify such a term.

[14] Ibid, Paragraph 26(5).

[15] Ibid, Paragraph 26(8).

[16] Although (each for slightly different reasons) both *EE Limited v Cooper* [2020] UKUT 214 (LC) and *EE Limited v 100 NOX SARL* [2022] UKUT 130 (LC) are cautionary tales against applying for interim code rights so early that you are not able to sufficiently evidence your application.

[17] Ibid, Paragraph 30(3). Code agreements conferring interim code rights do not continue automatically under Paragraph 30(2) of the Code. Paragraph 30 of the Code is considered in more detail in Chapter Eight.

[18] *EE Ltd v Aviva Investors Ground Rent Holdco Ltd* [2021] UKUT 0057 (LC) at [20].

its own, if a code operator does not have need of a 'full' agreement entered into under Paragraph 20.[19] [20]

Applications under Paragraph 26 of the Code have become very common not just to set up interim rights pending determination of an application under Paragraph 20, but as preliminary applications to enable code operators to undertake 'multi-skilled visits' ("**MSVs**") to properties so that they can perform surveys in order to determine whether land might be suitable for telecoms apparatus. The Tribunal has given guidance on applications under Paragraph 26 of the Code to enable MSVs on several occasions now,[21] and has stressed that in these more limited applications:

"The issues are usually quite narrow. They do not require extensive evidence. they do not require complicated statements of case which obscure the issues or elaborate bundles of documents. They ought to be capable of being conducted within a relatively restricted budget, proportionate to the matters in issue." [22]

---

[19] See *Cornerstone Telecommunications Infrastructure Ltd v University of London* [2019] EWCA Civ 2075. This provides some context for the decision (albeit not binding in England and Wales) in *British Telecommunications Plc v Morrison* [2020] 8 WLUK 259. One may serve a Paragraph 20 Notice for the purposes of an interim code rights application only that fails to include a term proposing consideration. That notice would not be valid for the purposes of a full code rights application, but could be for an interim code rights application.

[20] The Court of Appeal has warned against making successive applications for interim code rights and never applying for full code rights, which may be an abuse of process and ripe to be struck out: see *Cornerstone Telecommunications Infrastructure Ltd v University of London* [2019] EWCA Civ 2075 at [81].

[21] See, for example, *Cornerstone Telecommunications Infrastructure Limited v St Martins Property Investments Limited* [2021] UKUT 262 (LC) and *EE Limited v HSBC Bank Plc* [2022] UKUT 174 (LC), in particular in respect of the limited costs the parties should reasonably incur in these kinds of applications.

[22] [2021] UKUT 262 (LC), [44].

Applications Under Paragraph 27 of the Code: Temporary Code Rights

Paragraph 27 of the Code permits a code operator to apply to the Tribunal for an order imposing *"such temporary code rights as appear reasonably necessary for securing the objective…"* [23] that:

"until the proceedings under paragraph 20 and any proceedings under paragraph 40 are determined, the service provided by the operator's network is maintained and the apparatus is properly adjusted and kept in repair." [24]

The purpose of this objective, and of Paragraph 27 as a whole, is to protect the code operator's telecoms apparatus and network in-between the termination of a relevant code agreement, and the decision of the Tribunal as to whether it will either impose a Code agreement or permit the relevant person to enforce the removal of the relevant telecoms apparatus from their land. The right to remove telecoms apparatus is explored in Chapter Ten.

An order under Paragraph 27 can only be applied for where:

(1) A code operator has given a Paragraph 20 notice to the relevant person,[25] which requires the relevant person's agreement on a temporary basis in respect of a right which is to be exercisable in relation to telecoms equipment already installed on, under or over the land in question;[26] and

(2) The relevant person has the right to require the removal of the telecoms apparatus under Paragraph 37 or 40(1) but the code

---

[23] Communications Act 2003, Schedule 3A, Paragraph 27(2).

[24] Ibid, Paragraph 27(3).

[25] Ibid, Paragraph 27(1)(a).

[26] Ibid, Paragraph 27(1)(b).

operator is not for the time being required to remove the telecoms apparatus.[27]

And just as with applications under Paragraph 26:

(1) Paragraphs 22 to 25 and 84 of the Code all apply in applications under Paragraph 27;[28] and

(2) Orders can be made on applications made before the expiry of the twenty-eight-day period for Paragraph 20 notices *"if the court thinks that the order should be made as a matter of urgency."*[29]

Just as with code agreements conferring interim code rights, code agreements conferring temporary code rights will terminate without the need for further action following the decision of the Tribunal in the proceedings brought under either Paragraph 20 or 40 of the Code.[30]

Unlike in Paragraph 26, no specific provision is made in Paragraph 27 of the Code for temporary code rights to terminate on a certain date or event without the need for further action to be taken by either party. It would appear then that code agreements conferring temporary code rights must be terminated in the same manner as 'standard' code agreements imposed under Paragraph 20 of the Code.

---

[27] Ibid, Paragraph 27(1)(c).

[28] Ibid, Paragraph 27(4).

[29] Ibid, Paragraph 27(5).

[30] Ibid, Paragraph 30(3). Code agreements conferring temporary code rights do not continue automatically under Paragraph 30(2) of the Code. Paragraph 30 of the Code is considered in more detail in Chapter Eight.

The Applicable Test

The test to be applied by the Tribunal in an application under Paragraph 20 of the Code is set out in Paragraph 21:

"(1) Subject to sub-paragraph 5, the court may make an order under paragraph 20 if (and only if) the court thinks that both of the following conditions are met.

(2) The first condition is that the prejudice caused to the relevant person by the order is capable of being adequately compensated by money.

(3) The second condition is that the public benefit likely to result from the making of the order outweighs the prejudice to the relevant person.

(4) In deciding whether the second condition is met, the court must have regard to the public interest in access to a choice of high quality electronic communications services." [31]

These same conditions apply in respect of applications under Paragraph 26 of the Code, save that the Tribunal need only be satisfied that there is a *"good arguable case"* that they are made out.[32] The conditions are not relevant to applications under Paragraph 27, which fall to be determined in accordance with whether its unique objective would be secured by the grant.

Whereas the first condition requires the Tribunal to tread familiar legal ground (because there is ample guidance on whether interruption of use of land is capable of being adequately compensated in money in case law on the grant of injunctive relief), the second condition is likely to require expert evidence. In *EE Ltd and Hutchinson 3G UK Ltd v London Underground Ltd*,[33] which concerned an application for interim code rights over a building forming part of London Underground's

---

[31] Ibid, Paragraph 21(1) to (4).

[32] Ibid, Paragraph 26(3)(b).

[33] [2021] UKUT 142 (LC).

operational estate, the telecoms operators produced evidence from a chartered surveyor in respect of the *"difficulties which will be created for the coverage and capacity achievable by the claimants' mobile phone networks..."* should they not be granted the interim rights.[34]

And in determining the telecoms operators' interim rights application in <u>London Underground</u>, Martin Rodger QC made sure to highlight that *"the standard of proof will be different in any paragraph 20 application. Much more extensive rights would also be in issue and the concerns which* [the expert] *identifies in his evidence are likely to become even more acute."*[35]

The Redevelopment Defence

However, even if the above two conditions are satisfied, Paragraph 21(5) provides that:

"The court may not make an order under paragraph 20 if it thinks that the relevant person intends to redevelop all or part of the land to which the code right would relate, or any neighbouring land, and could not reasonably do so if the order were made."

This defence substantially mirrors Ground (f) of Section 30(1) of the Landlord and Tenant Act 1954 (**"the 1954 Act"**); in fact, it was deliberately modelled on it by the Law Commission, as explored by the Upper Tribunal in *EE Ltd v Chichester* [2019] UKUT 164 (LC).[36]

To that extent, the case law concerning Ground (f) will be of real assistance to relevant persons considering running this defence, albeit not strictly binding as *"the Code... must be looked at with a clean slate and as a fresh start. The principles relevant to the 1954 Act should be adopted where*

---

[34] Ibid, [10].

[35] Ibid, [12]. Also made clear by the Court of Appeal in <u>Cornerstone Telecommunications Infrastructure Ltd v University of London</u> [2019] EWCA Civ 2075 at [77].

[36] At [33].

they are relevant, although we are mindful of the need to be aware of different context in Code cases." [37]

It follows that the relevant person will need to establish in evidence both the settled intention to redevelop [38] and also that the redevelopment could not be reasonably carried out if the land in question were subject to the rights sought.[39] Redevelopment plans conceived purely to defeat a claim for code rights *"which the relevant person would not pursue if Code rights were not sought, will not satisfy the test in para.21(5)".*[40]

It should be noted that this defence forms part of Paragraph 21 of the Code, and so is not applicable to applications under Paragraph 27, which rise and fall on their own unique objective.

National Security

Section 66 of PSTIA (which is not yet in force at the time of publication) creates a new Paragraph 27ZA, enabling the refusal of an application on grounds of national security. The Tribunal is required to refuse the application if the Secretary of State gives a certificate to the court certifying that the Secretary of State is satisfied that the order applied for by the operator would be likely to prejudice national security, defence or law enforcement.

---

[37] [2019] UKUT 164 (LC) at [38].

[38] See e.g. *S Franses Ltd v Cavendish Hotel (London) Ltd [2018] UKSC 62* in respect of the requisite intention.

[39] See e.g. *Leathwods Ltd v Total Oil Great Britain Ltd* [1985] 51 P&CR 20 where the proposed works of reconstruction would make it impossible, both during the redevelopment and after it was complete, for the tenant to carry on his business from the premises.

[40] [2019] UKUT 164 (LC) at [39].

Summary

In summary:

(1) By virtue of the 2017 Regulations, *"the court"* under the Code will almost always be the Upper Tribunal, save in applications under Part 4A where it will be the First-tier Tribunal;

(2) Twenty-eight days after service of the Paragraph 20 notice, the code operator can apply to the Tribunal for it to impose code rights on the relevant person, if no agreement has been reached. The code operator can apply earlier if the relevant person writes to them making clear no agreement will be reached before the twenty-eight-day period expires;

(3) Code operators can apply to the Tribunal for it to impose interim code rights on the relevant person any time after service of a Paragraph 20 notice seeking interim code rights. An application made before the twenty-eight-day period expires will be entertained if sufficiently urgent. Interim code rights terminate without further action on the date, or after the event, prescribed by the Tribunal;

(4) Where there is already telecoms apparatus on the land, and the relevant person has the right to require it be removed, a code operator can serve a Paragraph 20 notice and then apply to the Tribunal for temporary code rights pending the determination of any application under Paragraph 20. An application made before the twenty-eight-day period expires will be entertained if sufficiently urgent;

(5) The Tribunal will impose code rights provided the telecoms operator can satisfy two conditions: (1) that any prejudice to the relevant person is capable of being adequately compensated in money, and (2) that the public benefit likely to arise from the making of the order outweighs the prejudice to the relevant person;

(6) Interim code rights will be imposed provided that the telecoms operator can show a good arguable case that those two conditions are made out;

(7) Neither code rights nor interim code rights will be granted if the relevant person can establish the defence that they intend to redevelop all or part of the land to which the code right(s) would relate, or any neighbouring land, and could not reasonably do so if the order were made;

(8) Soon, provision will come into effect requiring the Tribunal to refuse applications where national security is likely to be prejudiced, according to the relevant Secretary of State; and

(9) Whether temporary code rights are to be granted is subject to its own unique objective, namely whether the grant is reasonably necessary to secure the continued maintenance of the code operator's telecoms network, or the repair and adjustment of their apparatus, pending the outcome of their Paragraph 20 application.

CHAPTER FIVE

TERMS OF AND FORMALITIES FOR CODE AGREEMENTS, AND ENFORCEMENT

In this chapter, we explain:

(1) The terms that must be included in a code agreement imposed by the Tribunal;

(2) The Tribunal's discretion to include other terms in an imposed code agreement;

(3) The formalities required for a code agreement that has either been agreed or had its terms determined by the Tribunal; and

(4) How code agreements and code rights are enforced.

Mandatory Terms for Imposed Code Agreements

Whereas the Code does not limit the scope of the terms that can be included in code agreements entered voluntarily (save for the formalities considered below), Paragraph 23 of the Code outlines the scope of the terms that the Tribunal can impose:

"(1) An order under paragraph 20 may impose an agreement which gives effect to the code right sought by the operator with such modifications as the court thinks appropriate.

(2) An order under paragraph 20 must require the agreement to contain such terms as the court thinks appropriate, subject to sub-paragraphs (3) to (8).

(3) The terms of the agreement must include terms as to the payment of consideration by the operator to the relevant person for the relevant person's agreement to confer or be bound by the code right (as the case may be).

(4) Paragraph 24 makes provision about the determination of consideration under sub-paragraph (3).

(5) The terms of the agreement must include the terms the court thinks appropriate for ensuring that the least possible loss and damage is caused by the exercise of the code right to persons who—

(a) occupy the land in question,

(b) own interests in that land, or

(c) are from time to time on that land.

(6) Sub-paragraph (5) applies in relation to a person regardless of whether the person is a party to the agreement.

(7) The terms of the agreement must include terms specifying how long the code right conferred by the agreement is exercisable.

(8) The court must determine whether the terms of the agreement should include a term—

(a) permitting termination of the agreement (and, if so, in what circumstances);

(b) enabling the relevant person to require the operator to reposition or temporarily remove the electronic communications equipment to which the agreement relates (and, if so, in what circumstances)."

So, when considering what terms to impose on the parties, the Tribunal must both have regard to ensuring that the *"least possible loss and damage"* is caused by the grant,[1] and also (regardless of whether such terms are proffered in the Paragraph 20 notice) whether to impose terms relating to termination of the agreement and repositioning or removal of the telecoms apparatus.[2] In any event, the Tribunal must impose the payment of consideration [3] and specify the period for which the code right will be exercisable.[4]

Further, the Tribunal has the power to modify the code right sought in the Paragraph 20 notice, granting the code operator something different to what it sought,[5] and it must require the code agreement to contain any other terms that it thinks appropriate.[6]

Finally, it should be noted that all of the above also applies to any applications made under Paragraphs 26 and 27 of the Code in respect of interim or temporary code rights.[7]

Discretionary Terms for Imposed Code Agreements

The extent of the discretion to impose other terms on the code operator and relevant person under Paragraph 23(2) of the Code was considered by the Tribunal in *Cornerstone Telecommunications Infrastructure Ltd v Keast*.[8]

---

[1]   Communications Act 2003, Schedule 3A, Paragraph 23(5).

[2]   Ibid, Paragraph 23(8).

[3]   Ibid, Paragraph 23(3) and (4).

[4]   Ibid, Paragraph 23(7).

[5]   Ibid, Paragraph 23(1).

[6]   Ibid, Paragraph 23(2).

[7]   Ibid, Paragraphs 26(4)(c) and 27(4)(c).

[8]   [2019] UKUT 116 (LC).

In Cornerstone's Paragraph 20 notice it sought a number of terms be included in the proposed code agreement that were not code rights, including:

(1) Warranties and a covenant for quiet enjoyment to be entered by Mr Keast;

(2) The right for Cornerstone to install a generator on the relevant land;

(3) The right for Cornerstone to compel Mr Keast to enter into agreements with third parties, and to restrict his ability to negotiate with them;

(4) A right for Cornerstone to restrict Mr Keast's access to the relevant land;

(5) Covenants on the part of Mr Keast to maintain the condition of his farm and protect the land from interference;

(6) Covenants on the part of Mr Keast to notify Cornerstone of various matters;

(7) Covenants on the part of Mr Keast not to interfere with the relevant land or authorise any interference with it; and

(8) A restriction on Mr Keast's ability to develop other parts of his property.

The Tribunal considered the meaning and effect of Paragraph 23(2) of the Code, and concluded that:

"... paragraph 23 contains no restriction upon the terms that may be imposed, although sub-paragraphs (3) to (8) set out what they must include.

Clearly in deciding what it thinks appropriate the Tribunal will have very careful regard to the overall scheme of the Code, which provides for the imposition of Code rights and other terms on occupiers of land at a rate of consideration far lower than was payable under the old code. The Tribunal will have in mind the need to be fair to both parties, and what is "appropriate" is likely to be influenced by the basis of consideration that it can impose. It may be considered inappropriate to impose on a site provider certain obligations intended to facilitate the provision of the operator's network when the consideration receivable by the site provider is to be unrelated to the value of that network.

But there is no principled reason why there should not be, for example, a restriction on the landowner's right of access to the site, in the interests of safety, or a restriction on the landowner's ability to give others access to the site. Whether there is any scope for the imposition of positive obligations on the landowner is a difficult question and one might expect that it would be a rare occurrence. But it is not outside the Tribunal's jurisdiction. I see no reason to regard any terms to which the Respondent points as outside the Tribunal's jurisdiction, although there are some that it might well, in the exercise of its discretion, refuse to impose." [9]

As the *Keast* litigation concerned preliminary issues, rather than a final determination of the terms to be imposed, the Tribunal did not go on to specify which of the terms proposed by Cornerstone in its Paragraph 20 notice it would grant or refuse. However, the Tribunal's position on the scope of its discretion is clear: the discretion is wide, and how it is exercised is most likely to be informed by the nature of the consideration it can and will award under Paragraph 24 of the Code.[10]

The exercise of the discretion found in Paragraph 23(2) of the Code was also considered by the Tribunal in *Cornerstone Telecommunications Infrastructure Ltd v London and Quadrant Housing Trust*.[11] In that case, Cornerstone wanted to acquire code rights to install equipment on the roof of an eighty-storey block containing both offices and residential flats. The roof already housed solar panels, and the apparatus would be installed around them.

---

[9] Ibid, [56]-[58].

[10] For which, see Chapter Six.

[11] [2020] UKUT 282 (LC).

The housing trust was concerned about the effect of increased weight on the roof, and argued that the Tribunal should impose a term in the code agreement prescribing an 'equipment cap' limiting Cornerstone's code rights to protect the integrity of the building.[12] Further, Cornerstone argued that the wording of Paragraph 23(2) suggests (because the Tribunal should impose *"an agreement which gives effect to the code right sought by the operator…"*) that the starting point for the Tribunal should be the terms proposed by the code operator, and that the relevant person must justify any departure therefrom.

Dealing with these arguments in reverse, the Tribunal concluded that:

(1) The starting point for formulating the agreement to be imposed is the code right itself, which should not be modified unless the Tribunal considers it appropriate to do so under Paragraph 23(1). As for the other terms of the code agreement, these are subject to a wide discretion with no presumption in favour of the code operator's proposed terms;[13] and

(2) That the housing trust's fear that Cornerstone might install unlimited equipment on the roof of the building, threatening its integrity, was *"fanciful"* given that the agreed terms included a term prohibiting Cornerstone *"from overloading any part of the building, and requiring it to take all reasonable steps to ensure that it does not make the building or any plant or machinery on it unsafe"*.

The Tribunal also clarified that Paragraph 23(5) of the Code is not a *"prohibition on the imposition of code rights which may cause loss and damage to the owners and occupiers of land. It is a direction to the Tribunal to incorporate terms intended to minimise loss and damage as part of an agreement which will also include terms as to consideration assessed under*

---

[12] The issue of equipment caps have been something of a flashpoint for the exercise of the discretion at Paragraph 23(2) of the New Code, given that one was also argued for by the relevant person in *Cornerstone Telecommunications Infrastructure Ltd v University of the Arts London* [2020] UKUT 248 (LC): see e.g. [130].

[13] [2020] UKUT 282 (LC) at [43].

para.24 and rights to compensation for loss and damage for the site provider and others under paras 25, 44 and 84." [14] This approach to Paragraph 23(5) substantially mirrors the approach towards Paragraph 23(2) adopted in *Keast*.

More recently, the Tribunal has had to determine a number of references relating, broadly, to terms concerning site safety and liability for the same.

In *EE Ltd v Hackney LBC*,[15] the issue was whether indemnities given by code operators in code agreements should be general or restricted to claims by third parties. Martin Rodger QC found that *"when Parliament designed the Code it saw fit to confer on site providers a right of compensation and not a statutory Indemnity against all losses free of those restrictions. It cannot have considered that statutory compensation provided inadequate protection or have intended that paragraph 23(5) should oblige the Tribunal to impose an even more comprehensive contractual indemnity."* [16] The Deputy President was also persuaded by OFCOM's model form of code agreement, which contains only an indemnity clause limited to third party claims. He decided that the contractual indemnity should therefore be limited to third-party claims.

Subsequently, in *On Tower UK Ltd v AP Wireless II (UK) Ltd*,[17] the Tribunal was asked to determine whether terms should be included in a code agreement in order to protect or insulate the site provider from criminal or tortious liability as a result of the safety (or more precisely, the lack thereof) of telecoms equipment they were compelled to keep on their land. Cooke J held that the terms sought by the site provider were not appropriate as, on the facts before her, it would be the code operator

---

[14] Ibid, [48].

[15] [2021] UKUT 142 (LC).

[16] Ibid, [17].

[17] [2022] UKUT 152 (LC).

and not the site provider who would be liable under e.g. the Occupiers Liability Act 1957 or the Health and Safety at Work etc. Act 1974.[18]

Formalities for All Code Agreements

Regardless of whether a code agreement has been entered into freely by the code operator and the relevant person, or has had its terms imposed on them by the Tribunal, it must comply with all of the formalities set out in Paragraph 11 of the Code:

"(1) An agreement under this Part–

(a) must be in writing,

(b) must be signed by or on behalf of the parties to it,

(c) must state for how long the code right is exercisable, and

(d) must state the period of notice (if any) required to terminate the agreement." [19]

The Part of the Code this refers to is Part 2. Any code agreement entered into pursuant to the Code is considered to be an agreement under Part 2 of the Code.[20]

These formalities also apply to code agreements that have been varied, whether consensually or under Paragraph 34 of the Code:[21]

---

[18] See also the Tribunal-described 'sequel' case of *Cornerstone Telecommunications Infrastructure Limited v Hackney LBC* [2022] UKUT 210 (LC), which concerned who should have the last word as to the adequacy of risk assessments that were a pre-condition for the code operator utilising certain access rights.

[19] Communications Act 2003, Schedule 3A, Paragraph 11(1).

[20] This becomes relevant in the context of Part 5 of the Code (see Chapter Eight) and the transitional provisions between the Old Code and the Code (see Chapter Twelve).

[21] Variation of code agreements is considered in Chapter Twelve.

"(2) Sub-paragraph (1)(a) and (b) also applies to the variation of an agreement under this Part.

(3) The agreement as varied must still comply with sub-paragraph (1)(c) and (d)."[22]

The Code does not contain any express provision setting out the consequences of failing to comply with these formalities. Presumably, failure to comply with the formalities would render the agreement not *"An agreement under this Part"* i.e., not a code agreement. A potential consequence of this is considered below.

Given the lack of any prescribed standard form of code agreement (although OFCOM does publish model code agreements online), it is unsurprising that the Upper Tribunal has held that it is able to order that tripartite agreements be entered into between code operator, site provider and a relevant person under Paragraph 20(1)(b) of the Code.[23]

Enforcement of Code Rights and Agreements

Pursuant to Paragraph 93 of the Code:

"An agreement under this code, and any right conferred by this code, may be enforced–

(a) in the case of an agreement imposed by a court or tribunal, by the court or tribunal which imposed the agreement,

(b) in the case of any agreement or right, by any court or tribunal which for the time being has the power to impose an agreement under this code, or

(c) in the case of any agreement or right, by any court of competent jurisdiction."

---

[22] Communication's Act 2003, Schedule 3A, Paragraph 11(2)-(3).

[23] See *Vodafone Ltd v Gencomp (No. 7) Limited* [2022] UKUT 223 (LC).

It should be noted that Paragraph 93 of the Code is not drafted and/or. It therefore follows that:

(1) An imposed code agreement should be enforced in the court or tribunal that imposed it; else

(2) A code agreement entered voluntarily (or a code agreement imposed by a court or tribunal which is no longer extant) should be enforced in the court or tribunal with the power to impose code agreements; else

(3) Where there is no longer a court or tribunal with the power to impose code agreements, they should be enforced in any court of competent jurisdiction.[24]

In practice, by virtue of the 2017 Regulations,[25] code agreements and code rights whether entered voluntarily or imposed are likely to be enforceable in the Tribunal.

One situation where this would not be the case would be where a code agreement has been imposed in (for example) the county court, because the Tribunal opted to transfer an application under Paragraph 20 there pursuant to its power under Regulation 5 of the 2017 Regulations.

Another is where a code operator and relevant person have entered into an agreement that purports to be a code agreement but does not comply with all of the formalities contained in Paragraph 11 of the Code. If that agreement is not properly considered a code agreement as a consequence of that failure, it would not be enforceable under Paragraph 93 of the

---

[24] This analysis, although not yet tested in the Upper Tribunal or the courts, marries with Regulation 4 of the Electronic Communications Code (Jurisdiction) Regulations 2017 (SI 2017/1284), which (by virtue of Paragraph 93 being contained in Part 16 of the Code) does not mandate that enforcement applications under Paragraph 93 of the Code be brought in the Tribunal. So there must be some circumstances under which enforcement applications under the Code can be issued in an another forum.

[25] Electronic Communications Code (Jurisdiction) Regulations 2017 (SI 2017/1284). See Chapter Four.

Code. Instead, it would have to be enforced in any court with the requisite jurisdiction to determine contractual disputes generally.

Summary

In summary:

(1) The mandatory terms for imposed code agreements include payment of consideration and the period of the agreement. The Tribunal must also have regard to causing the least possible loss to the relevant person and other third parties (subject to the ability to order consideration and compensation be paid), and whether to include terms providing for early termination and the repositioning or removal of apparatus by either party;

(2) The Tribunal has a wide discretion to order that the code agreement contain other terms that it considers appropriate;

(3) All code agreements must comply with four core formalities. They must be in writing, be signed by or on behalf of the parties, state the period of the agreement, and state the period of notice require to terminate the agreement (if any); and

(4) In almost all cases, disputes related to the enforcement of extant code agreements under the Code fall under the jurisdiction of the Tribunal.

CHAPTER SIX

CONSIDERATION
AND VALUATION

This chapter considers four topics:

(1) The policy underpinning consideration under the Code

(2) The circumstances in which there is an obligation to pay consideration under the Code;

(3) The method of valuation of consideration under the Code; and

(4) The valuation of rent for telecoms equipment under Section 34 of the 1954 Act.[1]

It should be noted that compensation is not addressed in this chapter, but in Chapter Seven.

The Policy Underpinning Consideration Under the Code

In order to understand the approach taken to consideration in the Code it is necessary to consider the background against which the Code was drafted and the policy underpinning the code.[2] Ed Vaizey, the Minister of State for Culture and the Digital Economy confirmed in the forward to his ministerial statement in May 2016 '*A New Electronic Communications Code*':

"*It will make major reforms to the rights that communications providers have to access land – moving to a "no scheme" basis of valuation regime. This will*

---

[1]   Landlord and Tenant Act 1954.

[2]   For which generally, see Chapter One.

ensure property owners will be fairly compensated for use of their land, but also explicitly acknowledge the economic value for all of society created from investment in digital infrastructure. In this respect, it will put digital communications infrastructure on a similar regime to utilities like electricity and water. This will help deliver the coverage that is needed, even in hard to reach areas."

The May 2016 ministerial statement directly addressed the method of assessing consideration. In the section entitled '*Government response: How Consideration is to be Determined*' it was recorded that the Law Commission review in 2013 led to recommendations which were directed towards tackling '*ransom rents*'. The ministerial statement continued to note that while site providers should get "*fair value for the use of their land*" that "*this should not, as a matter of principle, include a share of the economic value created by very high public demand for services that the operator provides.*" As a result, the proposal was to limit consideration in the new scheme by adopting a 'no scheme' rule in order to "*encourage greater investment and improved network coverage.*"

The Obligation to Pay Consideration

The requirement to pay consideration differs depending on whether the parties have reached an agreement or referred the matter to the court.

Part 2 of the Code makes provision regarding the conferral of code rights, those who are bound by such rights and the exercise of code rights. When agreements are reached consensually pursuant to Part 2 of the Code, the formalities in Paragraph 11 of the Code must be completed.[3] But there is no provision there requiring the payment of consideration. In practice such compensation would usually be agreed.

Where no agreement is reached between the code operator and the relevant person, Part 4 of the Code confers power on the court to impose

---

3   For which, see Chapter Five.

an agreement.[4] When the matter is referred to the Tribunal, pursuant to Part 4 of the Code the obligation to pay consideration is mandatory.[5] By Paragraph 23(3) of the Code the agreement must provide terms for the payment of consideration by the operator to the relevant person in return for that person conferring or being bound by the code right.

By Paragraph 24(4) of the Code, the terms imposed by the court may be for consideration to be payable as a lump sum or periodically. Payment may also be on the occurrence of a specified event or events or otherwise as the Tribunal may direct.

The Valuation Method: the *London Borough of Islington* Case

As Part 2 of the Code is silent regarding consideration in cases in which an agreement has been reached, it follows that the parties can freely adopt whatever method of calculation they choose to calculate consideration.

In those cases where the powers of the court are invoked under Part 4 of the Code, there is no freedom to adopt the method of calculation the parties choose. Paragraph 24 of the Code specifies the formula for calculating consideration. That is the only formula which may be used and requires the valuation criteria and assumptions specified at Paragraph 24(1) to (3) of the Code to be utilised: see *EE Ltd and Hutchinson 3G Ltd v London Borough of Islington* [6] at [60].

---

[4]   For which, see Chapter Four.

[5]   Save that in applications for interim or temporary code rights, Paragraphs 26(6)(b) and 27(6)(b) change the inclusion of terms as to the payment of consideration from a *"duty"* to a *"power"*, meaning that in those kinds of applications such terms are not mandatory. This was explored by the Lands Tribunal (Scotland) in *British Telecommunications Plc v Morrison* [2020] 8 WLUK 259.

[6]   [2019] UKUT 53 (LC).

By Paragraph 24(1) of the Code, the consideration *"must be an amount or amounts representing the market value of the relevant person's agreement to confer or be bound by the code right (as the case may be)."*

This definition of *"market value"* departs from the usual definition of 'market rent', which was usually a price agreed by a willing buyer and willing seller in an arm's length transaction. Instead, this now focuses upon the value of the agreement to only one of the parties – the seller. This was considered by Martin Rodger QC in his judgment in <u>London Borough of Islington</u> at [60]-[62] and was described there as *"a surprising formulation"*.

In <u>London Borough of Islington</u> at [63], Martin Rodger QC considered whether there may have been an intention to signal an application of the principles used in compensation for compulsory purchase, namely that any value attributable solely to the scheme of the authority which proposed to acquire land compulsorily must be left out of account. This was the <u>Point Gourde</u> principle derived from the House of Lords decision in <u>Pointe Gourde Quarrying and Transport Co Ltd v Sub-Intendent of Crown Lands</u>.[7] This established that any additional value which was existed only because of the intention of the relevant authority was to be disregarded.

However, Paragraph 24(1) of the Code is subject to the detailed definition of *"market value"* in Paragraph 24(2) of the Code which provides that it is:

"For this purpose the market value of a person's agreement to confer or be bound by a code right is subject to sub-paragraph (3), the amount that, at the date the market value is assessed, a willing buyer would pay a willing seller for the agreement—

(a) in a transaction at arm's length,

---

[7]   [1947] AC 565.

(b) on the basis that the buyer and seller were acting prudently and with full knowledge of the transaction, and

(c) on the basis that the transaction was subject to the other provisions of the agreement imposed by the order under paragraph 20."

On this basis Martin Rodger QC considered it as giving *"an entirely conventional shape to the exercise"*,[8] citing Lord Hoffman in <u>IRC v Gray (Executor of Lady Fox)</u>:[9]

"It cannot be too strongly emphasised that although the sale is hypothetical, there is nothing hypothetical about the open market in which it is supposed to have taken place. The concept of the open market involves assuming that the whole world was free to bid, and then forming a view about what in those circumstances would in real life have been the best price reasonably obtainable..."

What is critical to the assessment is the introduction of the assumptions contained in Paragraph 24(3) of the Code, which requires that the market value *"must be assessed on these assumptions"*, namely:

"(a) that the right that the transaction relates to does not relate to the provision or use of an electronic communications network;

(b) that paragraphs 16 and 17 (assignment, and upgrading and sharing) do not apply to the right or any apparatus to which it could apply;

(c) that the right in all other respects corresponds to the code right;

(d) that there is more than one site which the buyer could use for the purpose for which the buyer seeks the right.

In <u>London Borough of Islington</u> at [66], the Tribunal described the first of these assumptions as *"the most significant"* and adopted the term the *"no-network"* assumption to describe it. The no-network assumption

---

8   [2019] UKUT 53 at [64].

9   [1994] STC 360.

eliminates any argument by the occupier that the compensation should be commensurate with the potential profit the code operator will make as a telecoms network provider. No value arising from the intention of the code operator to use the site as part of its network is permitted.[10] The relevant person is prevented from factoring in any ransom. This is extremely favourable to the code operator, and is a material and deliberate departure from the position prior to the Code.

The second assumption is that Paragraphs 16 and 17 of the Code do not apply.[11]

The third assumption is that the right in all other respects corresponds to the code right. In *London Borough of Islington* the Tribunal considered this assumption and held at [70] that:

"It has already been provided by para.24(2) that market value means the amount which would be agreed for rights conferred on the same terms as are provided for by the agreement being imposed, and it may therefore be that this assumption adds nothing of substance. It will be a question of fact in each case what use may be made of the site on the terms imposed, having regard to the no- network assumption. In this case the agreement to be imposed includes a covenant by the operator not to use the site other than for the permitted use of providing the networks of its shareholders. Despite the narrowness of the permitted use both parties approached the issue of valuation on the assumption that the rooftop site could be used for open storage. Once again, in this case we heard no evidence or detailed argument about para.24(3)(c) and we have reached no final conclusion on its potential effect, but we agree with the parties' implicit acknowledgement that the no-network assumption must permit some notional relaxation of contractual terms which would otherwise limit the permitted use to statutory Code purposes only. In principle, therefore, we do not think it is impermissible to have regard to rental values achieved for other uses even where the only permitted use under the imposed agreement is a Code use."

---

[10] See [2019] UKUT 53 at [68].

[11] For which, see Chapter Two.

The fourth and final assumption is that there is more than one site which the buyer could use. The purpose of this is to stop any monopoly of sites and prevent any impact on value to be caused by lack of suitable land.

In *London Borough of Islington*, the Tribunal reached a number of key conclusions on the approach to be taken to valuing the consideration under the Code:

(1) That there was no obligation upon the valuer to assume that the market in which the transaction occurs is competitive;[12]

(2) That the price was not necessarily nominal because there was only one bidder in the market;[13]

(3) The willing buyer cannot use the absence of demand to drive the price down to a level at which the seller would be not willing to transaction;[14]

(4) If the reality is that the nature of the premises is such that no one would pay anything for it then the market value may be nominal;[15] and

(5) That it was wrong to approach the assessment of consideration either on the basis that the absence of competition must necessarily result in a nominal value or that the assumption of a willing buyer would lead to a figure which was more than nominal.[16]

The Tribunal considered the value of the land in every case depended "*on its characteristics and potential uses and not simply on the number of*

---

[12] [2019] UKUT 53 at [83].

[13] Ibid, at [84] citing *FR Evans (Leeds) Ltd v English Electric Co Ltd* (1978) 36 P&CR 185 and *Raja Vyricherla Narayana Gajapatiraju v The Revenue Divisional Officer Vizagapotam* [1939] AC 302 at 316.

[14] [2019] UKUT 53 at [86].

[15] [2019] UKUT 53 at [87]-[90].

[16] Ibid, at [91].

potential bidders in the market." [17] The site provider in <u>London Borough of Islington</u> was be taken to be the landlord of all of the occupiers in the building and to owe contractual and statutory duties to them (and that such occupiers may not welcome telecommunications equipment on the roof, potentially creating an additional administrative burden for the landlord) because those were the facts on the ground in that case.[18]

It was necessary to give effect to the no-network assumption, which meant that the purpose for which the rights are granted was assumed to have nothing to do with the provision of or use of a telecoms network.[19] As a result, it was not appropriate to use transactions under the Old Code as comparables.[20] The Tribunal also held that there was no presumption of a minimum amount payable before the willing seller would sell because there was a need to assume a transaction,[21] and that there was no increased level of consideration to reflect the acquisition of a right to install up to three additional dish antennae in the future as this was contrary to the no-network assumption.[22] Although there was no demand for space on the roof of the ten-storey residential building for any commercial purpose unconnected to telecommunications, that did not dictate a nominal consideration.[23]

The Tribunal considered that the case was unlike the case of <u>Port of London Authority v Transport for London</u> [24] because a lease granting code

---

[17] Ibid.

[18] [2019] UKUT 53 at [93].

[19] Ibid, at [94].

[20] Ibid, at [95]. There were a number of reasons for this: this approach failed to apply the no-network assumption; was based upon a different statutory valuation hypothesis; were historic values; the use of indexation over such a long period of time was unreliable; the transactions relied upon were those in which the site provider was not represented.

[21] Ibid, at [96].

[22] Ibid, at [97].

[23] Ibid, at [98].

[24] [2008] RVR 93.

rights was not a freehold sale which divests the seller of all interest in the site. Rather, it restricted what the respondent may do with the building (for example the apparatus needed to be resituated during works to the roof) and so the additional risks and obligations that the relationship created for the site provider must be taken into account.[25]

The Tribunal also considered that the case was not like *Hoare v National Trust* [26] or *Telereal Trillium v Hewitt* [27] in which a notional letting transferred expensive liabilities from the landlord to the tenant. While the seller was assumed to be willing, it wanted the best price payable and since the inconvenience of the equipment being situated on the roof was not offset by any benefit it was likely that the parties would agree that this should be reflected in the compensation payable.[28]

The Tribunal did agree with both parties that the code operator should make a contribution towards the costs and expenses of running the building and complying with its obligations. However, it regarded this as consideration rather than as compensation.[29]

The Tribunal also held that the consideration figure should take into account the fact that the terms sought, and which the Tribunal was to impose, did not include an annual service charge, and that the consideration payable to offset this should be less than the sum paid by individual leaseholders since some of the services they enjoyed would not be used by the code operator; a contribution towards roof repairs could also be taken into account.[30]

---

[25] [2019] UKUT 53 at [99].

[26] (1999) 77 P&CR 366.

[27] [2018] EWCA Civ 26.

[28] [2019] UKUT 53 at [100].

[29] Ibid, at [101].

[30] Ibid, at [102]-[105].

In conclusion, by an application of the relevant factors, the Tribunal assessed the appropriate consideration to be just £1,000.00 per annum.

The Valuation Method: the Three-Stage Test

In *Cornerstone Telecommunications Infrastructure Ltd v London and Quadrant Housing Trust* [31] the Tribunal emphasised that certain matters would necessarily be included in most cases where consideration was being assessed, namely:

(1) The current or alternative (non-network) use value which required that the value of the site as part of an operator's network was to be disregarded, but not its value to any other potential tenant;

(2) The value to the tenant of any additional benefits conferred by the letting; and

(3) The expense to the site provider of the operator using the site for the apparatus which could form additional consideration or compensation.[32]

This three-stage test was subsequently approved in *On Tower UK Ltd v J H and F W Green Ltd*.[33] The case involved the first decision under the Code of a valuation of a rural greenfield site. The site was located on an estate which had mixed use of residential and agricultural buildings. The Claimant was holding over and the Tribunal had to consider whether

---

[31] [2020] UKUT 282 (LC).

[32] Ibid,[93]-[94], [134]-[137]. These three principles were the first three of the six identified in by Martin Rodger QC (sitting as a judge In the County Court) in *Vodafone Ltd v Hanover Capital Ltd* [2021] 2 P&CR 3, which concerned a determination as to the rent payable under a lease renewed under Part II of the 1954 Act that conveyed code rights. The latter three stages were not considered relevant because compensation could be awarded under the Code for legal expenses and rent negotiations, and no addition to reflect inducement was permissible under the Code. *Hanover Capital* is considered further below.

[33] [2020] UKUT 348 (LC), at first instance. The appeal in [2021] EWCA Civ 1858 did not concern the consideration payable.

equipment and sharing rights should be limited and the annual rent. The Tribunal considered that the annual rent for the site was £1200 to reflect the proximity of residential buildings. It would have been £750 without the proximity of the residential buildings.

The Valuation Method: Modern Practice

In *EE Ltd v Affinity Water Ltd* [34] the Tribunal indicated that it would now rarely be necessary to adopt the *London and Quadrant* three-stage test because the levels of consideration under the code were clear. A number of decisions now gave broad guidance on the level of consideration under the Code that parties could expect the Tribunal to adopt in the absence of special features or particular sensitivities.[35]

A table was set out in *Affinity Water*,[36] and provided as follows:

Decision	Type of property	Annual consideration
CTIL v Fothringham (Lands Tribunal for Scotland)	Rural, estate location	£600 (£1,500 in year of installation)
On Tower v Green	Rural, adjacent to housing	£1,200
Marks & Spencer	City, department store/offices	£3,850
London & Quadrant	City, residential rooftop	£5,000

[2022] UKUT 8 (LC); [2022] L&TR14.

[35] Ibid, [31]-[34].

[36] Ibid, [31].

It should be noted that the Tribunal considered that there were dangers in using comparable transactions involving consensual agreements, which were often protected by confidentiality agreements and were difficult to analyse when disclosed as well as not concerning statutory compensation rights.[37]

This approach has been followed in later cases, such as *EE Ltd v Stephenson*,[38] in which the Tribunal repeated the guidance given in *Affinity Water*: "*evidence of real-world transactions for telecommunications sites is not promising material on which to base a valuation under paragraph 24*".[39] The Tribunal confirmed that reliance on negotiated Code transactions could not be justified and that in future parties should avoid adducing evidence of real world telecommunications transactions when the relevant assessment was being undertaken under Paragraph 24 of the Code.[40]

In *On Tower UK Ltd v AP Wireless II (UK) Ltd*,[41] the Tribunal considered the alternative use value and emphasised that whether it was high or low this value would always be relevant.[42] The Tribunal emphasised that the policy of the Code was not that site providers should get no value at all for their land and that Paragraph 24 operated on the basis that the site provider could let the site for some other use than telecommunications.

In this case, the valuation evidence was prepared prior to the decision in *Affinity Water* and supplemented by reports which considered that decision. The stance of the experts were that the three sites they considered were so different from that in the *Affinity Water* table that further analysis based on the three-stage test was required. The Tribunal noted that the comparable transactions the experts used relating to

---

37 Ibid, [35].

38 [2022] UKUT 180 LC.

39 Ibid at [58].

40 Ibid at [58]-[71].

41 [2022] UKUT 152 (LC)

42 Ibid at [228]-[229].

consensual transactions and, in the case of one expert, on the basis of the principles of the Old Code and repeated that the Tribunal has said on more than one occasion that such comparables were useless.[43] The Tribunal emphasised:

"As we said above, we do not believe that either the parties or the Tribunal will be assisted in future by evidence of consensual transactions for use as comparables, nor by argument about the small sums that might feature in a Hanover calculation. In most cases the [Affinity Water] table will remain a good indication of the level of consideration which would be agreed in the open market for sites with comparable characteristics let on the paragraph 24 assumptions, and it will not be difficult – as the valuers in these references eventually found – to fit new types of sites into that scale. To be blunt, it should be obvious that a ground level site in a car park or a haulage yard is going to command a higher rent than a rural site but less than a rooftop site or the top of a water tower. Valuation evidence, if it is needed at all in future references, ought to become a great deal simpler in light of the guidance that the Tribunal has now given."[44]

It appears then that, albeit having taken pains initially to fully conceptualise how consideration should be assessed under the Code, the Tribunal is now distancing itself from detailed consideration of the principles underlying its earlier decisions in favour of using the end result of those decisions as an indicator of what ought to be the appropriate consideration. Whilst this makes practical sense, as it will reduce the time and cost involved in making consideration determinations, it remains to be seen whether this rough-and-ready approach will stand up to scrutiny on appeal.

---

43 Ibid at [236].

44 Ibid at [257].

The Valuation of Rent for Telecoms Equipment Under Section 34 of the 1954 Act (pre-PSTIA)

In _Hanover Capital_, a subsisting agreement [45] was protected under Part 2 of the 1954 Act, and so the new rent had to be determined in accordance with Section 34 of the 1954 Act rather than the Code. So, the court was required to consider the rent in the open market, there being disregarded any effect on rent of Vodafone's occupation, goodwill attributable to its business, and improvements. The key valuation assumptions were:

(1) That the site was in the condition it was in _"if the actual tenant had removed fixtures installed by it and complied with its obligations"_ and _"as it was before the... lease was granted"_;[46]

(2) That the hypothetical tenant was a code operator _"because the terms of the tenancy say so and the only permitted use of the Site under those terms is for Code purposes"_;[47]

(3) That both negotiating parties were prudent and knowledgeable, including of the hypothetical tenant's rights under the Code;[48]

(4) The rent would be the only quantified sum payable;[49]

(5) The negotiation would be fair and friendly. The parties were assumed to be willing but not anxious to do a deal;[50] and

(6) It was noted that the process for negotiating terms for mast sites was fundamentally different to other property transactions, and that the real-world market was not the open market required under Section

---

[45] For which, see Chapter Twelve.

[46] [2021] 2 P&CR 3 at [50].

[47] Ibid, at [51].

[48] Ibid, at [51]-[52].

[49] Ibid, at [54].

[50] Ibid, at [57].

34 of the 1954 Act.[51] The non-network assumption required by Paragraph 24 of the Code formed the backdrop to the hypothetical negotiations.[52]

And the following six topics were considered *a "helpful framework"* in replicating the factors that would influence the parties in a case like *Hanover Capital*:[53]

(1) The alternative use value of the site which would be the equivalent of the rental value of the site for the most valuable non-operator use;

(2) An allowance to reflect any additional benefit conferred on the tenant by the letting;

(3) An adjustment to reflect any greater adverse effect of the letting on the willing lessor than the alternative use on which the existing use value was based;

(4) The fees payable by the hypothetical landlord for negotiating the rent with the hypothetical tenant's representatives;

(5) Conveyancing legal fees; and

(6) The possibility that the hypothetical tenant would pay an additional sum to induce the landlord to enter into the letting.[54]

Since this decision, however, doubt has been cast on how often the *Hanover Capital* structured approach will now need to be adopted in determining rents under Section 34 of the 1954 Act. In *EE Ltd v*

---

[51] Ibid, at [69]-[71].

[52] Ibid, at [87].

[53] The first three of which being adopted in *Cornerstone Telecommunications Infrastructure Ltd v London and Quadrant Housing Trust* [2020] UKUT 282 (LC) as the now (likely) defunct three-stage test, for which see above.

[54] [2021] 2 P&CR 3 at [89].

Morriss,[55] Martin Rodger QC (sitting as a judge of the County Court) gave the following view:

"where a rent is to be determined under section 34 of the 1954 Act the adoption of the structured approach resorted to in Hanover Capital is only necessary where reliable transactional evidence is missing... If the evidence of new lettings of bare sites is of sufficient quality and quantity to enable clear conclusions to be drawn... it is unnecessary to adopt the structured approach previously identified." [56]

It therefore appears that *Hanover Capital*, which at one point set out a necessary structure for determining rent in a national market sorely lacking relevant transactional evidence, will fade in relevance as more and more relevant lettings are agreed or determined, increasing the amount of available market evidence.[57]

Amendments Under PSTIA

Section 61 of the Product Security and Telecommunications Infrastructure Act 2022 ("**PSTIA**") is not yet in force and at the time of publication it is not known when it is due to be in force. However, it must be noted that it amends the 1954 Act by adding a new Section 34A in relation to a subsisting agreement where the primary purpose of the current tenancy is to confer code rights.

In default of an agreement, the rent payable granted by the court under the 1954 Act is *"the market value of the landlord's agreement to confer the code rights by the new tenancy"*. This is based on assumptions including

---

[55] [2023] 1 P&CR 7.

[56] Ibid at [88].

[57] Indeed, Martin Rodger QC followed his own approach from *EE Ltd v Morriss* [2023] 1 P&CR 7 more recently in *On Tower UK Ltd v AP Wireless II (UK) Ltd* [2022] 8 WLUK 155, where he was again sitting as a judge of the County Court.

the 'no code' assumption and other assumptions consistent with the broad approach to consideration under the Code.

Under Section 65 of PSTIA,[58] there is a further amendment by way of a new Section 32A to the 1954 Act to make regulations enabling the jurisdiction of the court under Part 2 of the 1954 Act to be exercised by the First-tier Tribunal or the Upper Tribunal in a case where the current tenancy is a subsisting agreement [59] within the meaning of Schedule 2 to the Digital Economy Act 2017, and the primary purpose of the current tenancy is to confer Code rights.

Summary

In summary:

(1) The policy objective of an expansion of the network coverage is critical to understanding and applying the Code;

(2) The parties are free to reach agreements under Part 2 of the Code as long as the formalities in Paragraph 11 are completed. When they do so they are free to agree the payment of consideration, and usually do so, although it is not mandatory;

(3) Where no agreement is reached the Tribunal has power to impose an agreement. In such cases there is an obligation to pay consideration. Consideration may be paid as a lump sum, periodically or on occurrence of a particular event;

(4) Under Part 2 of the Code the parties can adopt whatever method of valuation they wish to adopt. Under Part 4 of the Code the calculation specified in Paragraph 24 must be used, which includes a series of assumptions including the no-network assumption, and

---

[58] Which is in force pursuant to s79(1)(c) of PSTIA.

[59] For which, see Chapter Twelve.

assumption that more than one site can be used thus preventing the site provider from obtaining a ransom; and

(5) The Tribunal has now given sufficient guidance on the levels of consideration which are appropriate under the Code, and which will be adopted in the absence of special features. The table contained In *Affinty Water* is now the dominant indicator of appropriate consideration;

(6) In most cases under Paragraph 24, evidence of consensual real world transactions will not assist and should not be adduced;

(7) Under the 1954 Act, subsisting agreements to which Section 34 applies will have their rents assessed in the context of the Code's valuation principles and assumptions. For a time, in the absence of much 'Code-world' market evidence, this required detailed consideration of the principles set out in *Hanover Capital*. Now, with 'Code-world' market evidence more readily available, *Hanover Capital* is likely to fade in significance; and

(8) Once the PSTIA amendments come into effect, valuation of rents for subsisting agreements under the 1954 Act will even more closely mirror the approach under the Code. The Tribunal now has the jurisdiction to determine these claims.

CHAPTER SEVEN

COMPENSATION

This chapter considers nine topics:

(1) The power to award compensation under the Code;

(2) The order for compensation;

(3) The timing of the award for compensation;

(4) The limitation on compensation;

(5) The heads of compensation;

(6) Legal and valuation expenses;

(7) Diminution in value;

(8) Other claims for compensation; and

(9) Evidence.

It should be noted that consideration is not addressed in this chapter, but in Chapter Six.

The Power to Make an Order for Compensation

The parts of the Code which deal with compensation are Paragraph 25 and Part 14, which contains Paragraphs 83 to 86 of the Code.

By Paragraph 25(1) of the Code the Tribunal may make an order requiring the operator to pay compensation to the relevant person for any loss and damage which has been sustained or will be sustained by that person as a result of the code right to which the order relates.

Accordingly, the power of the Tribunal to order compensation is dependent on the order being made pursuant to Paragraph 20.

Part 14 of the Code makes additional provision regarding compensation. Paragraph 84(1) provides that Paragraph 84 of the Code applies in two circumstances:

(1) Where the power of the court is exercised pursuant to Paragraph 25(1) of the Code, imposing a code agreement on a person; and

(2) Where the power is exercised in Paragraph 44(5) of the Code for compensation in relation to the removal of apparatus from the land.[1]

Paragraph 84 of the Code does not apply where there is a consensual agreement to confer Code rights pursuant to Part 2.[2]

Part 14 of the Code also makes provision for compensation for injurious affection to neighbouring land in a case where an operator exercises a right conferred by Parts 2 to 9 of the Code.[3] The compensation is payable under Section 10 of the Compulsory Purchase Act 1965, and is payable irrespective of whether the person claiming the compensation has any interest in the land. The compensation is payable in relation to loss or damage sustained as a result of the code operator exercising code rights.

In _EE Ltd and Hutchinson 3G Ltd v London Borough of Islington_ [4] the Tribunal considered that the provisions of the Code relating to consideration were "_very flexible_". However, the Tribunal rejected a submission that the power was also discretionary. The Tribunal considered that the provisions of Paragraph 25 of the Code were

---

[1] For which, see Chapter Ten.

[2] Confirmed by the Tribunal in _EE Ltd and Hutchinson 3G Ltd v London Borough of Islington_ [2019] UKUT 53 at [144].

[3] Parts 7 to 9 falling outside the scope of this book. Also see _Elite Embroidery Ltd v Virgin Media Ltd_ [2018] UKUT 364 (LC) where a compensation claim brought under the Code failed because it did not relate to rights conferred under Parts 2 to 9 of the Code.

[4] [2019] UKUT 53.

expressed in terms which reflected the fact that in certain cases no compensation was required because there was no loss or damage sustained as a result of the exercise of code rights.[5] But where loss or damage was sustained the Tribunal did not consider that relief could be refused.

The Order for Compensation

By Paragraph 25(3) of the Code, the order for compensation may either specify the amount of compensation to be paid to the code operator or give directions for determination of the amount.

The directions may provide for the amount of the compensation to be agreed between the code operator and the relevant person, or for the dispute about quantum to be determined by arbitration.[6] Further, pursuant to Paragraph 25(5) of the Code, the code operator may be required to make the payment in a number of different ways: by a lump payment; periodic payments; a payment "*on the occurrence of an event or events*"; and there is also a broad power to order that payment be made "*in such other form or at such other time or times as the court may direct.*"

The Timing of the Award

Once the power is triggered it can be exercised either at the time an order under Paragraph 20 is made, or at any time afterwards on the application of the relevant person.[7]

In <u>*London Borough of Islington*</u>, the Tribunal rejected a submission that the award of compensation may only be made at the time the order imposing the code agreement was made. The Tribunal considered that this was contrary to the intention of Paragraph 25(2)(b) of the Code,

---

[5]   Ibid, at [109].

[6]   Communications Act 2003, Schedule 3A, Paragraph 25(4).

[7]   Ibid, Paragraph 25(2).

which allowed the order to be made "*at any times afterwards*", and contrary to the intended flexibility of the Code.[8] Further, the Tribunal considered that this would have the unjust consequence of meaning the site provider had to shoulder the burden of any unanticipated loss.

Limitation on Compensation

Under Paragraph 86 of the Code, provided the code operator is lawfully exercising rights conferred by the Code, it is protected from liability for loss and damage caused by the lawful exercise of any right conferred by the Code, except as provided by the Code. While this apparently prohibits any claims for compensation, save under the Code, it should be noted that this is expressly in relation to "*lawful*" exercise of rights.

We anticipate that there may be arguments about compensation in cases in which it is alleged that there was an unlawful exercise of rights, and what constitutes the "*unlawful*" use of code rights in due course. We predict that there are two potential ways in which the courts might interpret seek to Paragraph 86:

(1) Purposively, maintaining that a high threshold is required to consider that conduct of an operator was "*unlawful*" such that the limitation upon seeking compensation would not apply. This is because, as stated repeatedly by the courts in a number of cases considered in this book, the Code is intended to be a comprehensive scheme; or

(2) Strictly, such that any (for example) breach of contract is an "*unlawful*" act. This would mean that a code operator who exercises a code right in a manner prohibited under the code agreement (such as where a code right is only exercisable between certain hours of the day) and causes loss to the site provider by doing so would in principle be liable to compensate the site provider in damages for breach of contract.

---

8   [2019] UKUT 53 at [111].

Which approach will be adopted by the courts remains to be seen.

It should also be noted that there is no right to double recovery. It is clear from _London Borough of Islington_ that double counting is not permissible.[9] So, matters taken into account under the heading of consideration may not be claimed a second time as compensation. This is particularly pertinent to diminution in value (for which, see below). In _London Borough of Islington_ it was held that the site provider was not entitled to compensation for diminution in value of the land. Rather, that sum should be reflected in the consideration payable; only to the extent that such diminution is not so reflected can a separate claim be made for compensation.

Heads of Compensation

The heads of compensation in Paragraph 84(2) of the Code depend upon the circumstances of the case. But the power extends to:

"(a) expenses (including reasonable legal and valuation expenses, subject to the provisions of any enactment about the powers of the court by whom the order for compensation is made to award costs...

(b) diminution in value of the land, and

(c) costs of reinstatement." [10]

In _London Borough of Islington_ the Tribunal considered Paragraph 84(2) of the Code and stated at [117]:

"it is apparent that the list is not intended to be exhaustive: the power to order compensation "includes power" to order payment for the matters identified. In this case the relevant power is under para.25(1), which, in apparently unrestricted terms, confers jurisdiction to "order the operator to pay

---

[9]   Also see _Cornerstone Telecommunications Infrastructure Ltd v London & Quadrant Housing Trust_ [2020] UKUT 0282 (LC) at [99].

[10]   Communications Act 2003, Schedule 3A, Paragraph 84(2).

compensation to the relevant person for any loss or damage that has been sustained or will be sustained by that person as a result of the exercise of the code right". The reference in para.25 to "any loss or damage", the inclusive list of examples in para.84(2), and the incorporation of only some of the heads of compensation available under s.5 of the Land Compensation Act 1961, all suggest that other types of loss or damage may be capable of being the subject of compensation under para.25. It was however suggested ...that the only right to compensation was under the headings in para.84(2), but our provisional view is that that is too narrow an approach. It is not necessary for us to reach a concluded view on that question in this reference and we therefore prefer to leave it for consideration on an occasion when it can be fully argued."

Legal and Valuation Expenses

In *London Borough of Islington* it was not disputed that the site provider was entitled to reasonable legal and valuation expenses in connection with agreeing the Code agreement and for the temporary use of its land at ground level for a working compound.

The Tribunal noted that no attempt had been made to quantify the legal and valuation expenses.[11] It accepted that the recoverable fees were those incurred in seeking to agree terms for a code agreement and do not include costs incurred in resisting the agreement in principle or to compromise the reference itself. Those matters were decisions for the Tribunal as costs of the reference, as made clear by Martin Rodger QC in *London Borough of Islington* at [94]:

"Where a new letting is imposed by the Upper Tribunal on a reference under the Code the landlord is entitled, as a matter of law, to ask the tribunal to order a payment of compensation equal to its reasonable legal and valuation expenses (para.84(2)(a)). It is to be expected that such compensation will be ordered as a matter of routine, as it is in compulsory purchase cases, and that expectation is the basis of the universal practice concerning contributions to

---

[11] [2019] UKUT 53 at [122].

fees on new lettings and renewals. The willing landlord would be aware both of the right and of the practice, in the same way as it would be aware of the basis on which the tribunal would assess a rent. Mr Stott's approach to valuation assumes that the parties would conduct their rent negotiation with a view to mirroring the basis of valuation under the Code, and would therefore reach agreement on a rent reflecting the "no network" assumption. For the same reason the parties would agree that, since no fees are in fact to be paid under the terms they have settled on, an equivalent annual allowance ought to be included in the rent. That allowance, as Mr Jourdan agreed, should be £445."

In *Cornerstone Telecommunications Infrastructure Ltd v London & Quadrant Housing Trust* [12] the only compensation payable was the £3,068 reasonable legal expenses in advising on and completing the agreement a sum which did not include the costs incurred in respect of the proceedings. The Tribunal rejected a suggestion by the operator that the sum payable should be £3000 on the basis that there was no reason not to award the sum actually incurred.

Diminution in Value

Paragraph 84(3) of the Code applies *"rules (2) to (4) set out in section 5 of the Land Compensation Act 1961"* for the purpose of assessing diminution in value of the land in relation to England and Wales, which provide as follows:

"(2) The value of land shall, subject as hereinafter provided, be taken to be the amount which the land if sold in the open market by a willing seller might be expected to realise.

(2A) The value of land referred to in rule (2) is to be assessed in the light of the no-scheme principle set out in section 6A.

(3) The special suitability or adaptability of the land for any purpose shall not be taken into account if that purpose is a purpose to which it could

---

[12] [2020] UKUT 0282 (LC).

be applied only in pursuance of statutory powers, or for which there is no market apart from the requirements of any authority possessing compulsory purchase powers.

(4) Where the value of the land is increased by reason of the use thereof or of any premises thereon in a manner which could be restrained by any court, or is contrary to law, or is detrimental to the health of the occupants of the premises or to the public health, the amount of that increase shall not be taken into account."

There is a contrast between the assessment of consideration [13] and compensation because the assumptions and disregards under Paragraph 24 of the Code do not apply when assessing compensation under Paragraphs 25(1) and 84(2)(b) of the Code.

In *London Borough of Islington*, the Tribunal considered that the policy of a reduction of costs in providing high quality telecommunications service was apparent in the no-network assumption in Paragraph 24, but was not a policy which had the same impact in relation to the assessment of compensation.[14] However, the Tribunal also considered that it was not Parliament's intention to give the economic value that had been denied under the new consideration scheme in the form of compensation for diminution in value of the land.[15] The Tribunal noted that there was a distinction between compensation for diminution in the value of the land and consideration.[16] Consideration is a one-off periodic payment for grant of the right, while compensation was:

"recompense for loss or damage suffered by the site provider as a consequence of the agreement reached or imposed; it is the monetary equivalent of the loss or damage sustained. A site provider which allows its land to be occupied and which receives in return the market value of that occupation on a periodic

---

13 For which, see Chapter Six.

14 [2019] UKUT 53 (LC) at [130].

15 Ibid, at [131].

16 Ibid, at [132].

basis does not suffer loss or damage from being kept out of the use of the land or from being deprived of the opportunity to let it to someone else." [17]

The Tribunal acknowledged that the valuation assumptions prevented the site provider from realising recovering the true value of the land, and that this did not give rise to a loss for which compensation was payable under Paragraph 84 of the Code and did not, without more, give rise to loss or damage.[18] The Tribunal considered that the diminution in the value of the land was capable of being reflected in the consideration payable under Paragraph 24 of the Code. However, it was accepted that if it could be shown that the value of the land had been diminished to a greater extent than had been reflected in the assessment of consideration a separate claim may be admissible.[19]

Finally, the Tribunal noted that there could be circumstances in which the fact that the rights were to be used for the purpose of the electronic communications network (a factor disregarded in assessing compensation) could lead to a diminution in the value of the land. Further, circumstances occurring at a later date may result in an additional loss which was not anticipated when consideration was assessed which it was considered likely to be admissible in principle.[20]

The above statements of principle found support In *EE Ltd v Stephenson and AP Wireless II (UK) Ltd*.[21] In that case, the compensation claim went further than in *London Borough of Islington* as it concerned injurious affectation to land neighbouring the site over which code rights were to be granted over which the second respondent had a leasehold interest.

The Tribunal found that the suggestion that such injury would be caused was inchoate at such an early stage: *"To determine the suggestion of a claim at this stage could only result in its dismissal. The better course is to make no*

---

[17] Ibid.

[18] Ibid, at [133].

[19] Ibid, at [134].

[20] Ibid at [135].

[21] [2022] UKUT 180 (LC).

93

determination and to leave APW to make such further compensation claim as may be advised at a time of its choosing." [22] It remains to be seen whether such a compensation claim will be made in future.

Other Claims for Compensation

In *London Borough of Islington*, the Council put forward 29 separate claims for compensation on a variety of bases. This included 16 claims where a disturbance might be caused. The Tribunal rejected all of the claims for compensation save for the claims for legal and surveying costs and damage flowing from the installation of the apparatus.[23] A number of the claims were regarded as double counting because they were matters in respect of which consideration was payable, and others were unnecessary because they were already dealt with under the terms of the imposed agreement or dispute resolution provisions.[24]

Evidence for Compensation Claims

The quality of the evidence of loss will be of critical importance to the Tribunal. The valuation evidence in *London Borough of Islington* was described by the Tribunal in *London & Quadrant Housing Trust* as having been *"rudimentary"* as compared with the more detailed evidence in *Vodafone Ltd v Hanover Capital Ltd*,[25] in which there was evidence of the behaviour of professionally advised parties negotiating in the real market, and in which it was apparent where the no-network assumption had been taken into account. The Tribunal emphasised that *"the loss and damage anticipated in any particular case will depend on the characteristics of the*

---

[22] Ibid, [79].

[23] [2019] UKUT 53 (LC), [136]-[144].

[24] The position in relation to the claims was prepared prior to the final terms of the agreement being known and so the position regarding double counting and unnecessary terms were largely as a result of this and acknowledged in written submissions.

[25] [2021] 2 P&CR 3.

particular site." [26] The site provider should be prepared to adduce expert evidence and pertinent evidence of specific losses.[27]

Amendments Under PSTIA

Section 63 of the Product Security and Telecommunications Act 2022 ("**PSTIA**") is not yet in force and at the time of publication it is not known when it is due to be in force. However, it should be noted that it amends the Landlord and Tenant Act 1954 ("**the 1954 Act**")

by adding a new s34B in relation to a subsisting agreement where the primary purpose of the current tenancy is to confer code rights. The Tribunal may order the tenant to pay compensation to the landlord for any loss or damage which has been or will be sustained. The powers of the Tribunal mirror those in other situations, including the right to make such an order at the time the tenancy is granted or afterwards on the application of the landlord. The order may specify the amount of compensation or make directions for determining compensation to be agreed or determined by arbitration. The payments may be by a lump sum, periodical, contingent on an event or in such other form as the Tribunal directs. The compensation may include expenses, diminution in the value of the land or reinstatement.

Summary

In summary:

(1) Where there is an agreement to confer rights under the Code by consent under Part 2, the Tribunal has no power to order compensation under Paragraph 84 of the Code;

---

26   [2020] UKUT 0282 (LC) at [102].

27   It was in part this total lack of evidence that saw the Tribunal make no determination on compensation for injurious affectation of neighbouring land in *EE Ltd v Stephenson and AP Wireless II (UK) Ltd* [2022] UKUT 180 (LC).

(2) Under Paragraph 25 of the Code, the power of the Tribunal to award compensation is dependent upon an order being made by Paragraph 20, and Part 14 of the Code applies if the power of the Tribunal is exercised pursuant to Paragraph 25 or where exercised in relation to Paragraph 44(5) for removal of apparatus;

(3) When the Tribunal has power to make an order for compensation, that power is flexible but not discretionary providing loss and damage has been sustained;

(4) An order for compensation may specify the amount or give directions for determination of the amount including a direction for the dispute about quantum to be agreed or referred to arbitration;

(5) There is no restriction on when compensation can be ordered if the power to compensate is triggered;

(6) The operator may not be subject to a claim for compensation save under the Code, providing it is lawfully exercising its rights;

(7) Double recovery is impermissible. If a matter is taken into account in relation to consideration it may not also be the subject of an award of compensation;

(8) The heads of compensation include reasonable legal and valuation expenses, which will not include the costs of proceedings in the Tribunal;[28]

(9) Compensation will include diminution in value of the land unless already reflected in the consideration payable;

(10) Any other matters which were already addressed under the terms of the agreement, or dispute resolution mechanism, will not be taken into account; and

---

[28] For which, see Chapter Fourteen.

(11) Once amendments made to the 1954 Act by PSTIA come into force, compensation may also be claimed for thereunder in similar circumstances for subsisting agreements.[29]

---

[29] For which, see Chapter Twelve.

CHAPTER EIGHT

PART 5 OF THE CODE, AND THE CONTINUATION AND TERMINATION OF CODE AGREEMENTS TO WHICH IT APPLIES

In this chapter we address:

(1) The application of Part 5 of the Code;

(2) The continuation of code agreements to which Part 5 of the Code applies; and

(3) The termination of code agreements, to which Part 5 of the Code applies, by –

(a) Site provider giving notice under Paragraph 30 of the Code,

(b) Code operators, and

(c) Consent.

The Application of Part 5 of the Code

Paragraph 28 of the Code explains that Part 5 deals with:

"(a) the continuation of rights after the time at which they cease to be exercisable under an agreement,

(b) the procedure for bringing an agreement to an end,

(c) the procedure for changing an agreement relating to code rights, and

(d) the arrangements for the making of payments under an agreement whilst disputes under this Part are resolved."

The matters referred to in Paragraphs 28(a) and (b) of the Code are dealt with below in this chapter, whereas Paragraphs 28(c) and (d) of the Code are considered in Chapter Nine.

Pursuant to Paragraph 29(1) of the Code, Part 5 applies to *"an agreement under Part 2 of this code"*[1] subject to Paragraphs 29(2) to (4).[2] These sub-paragraphs in turn provide that Part 5 of the Code does not apply to a lease of land in England and Wales if its primary purpose is not to grant code rights and is one to which Part 2 of the 1954 Act:[3]

(1) Applies, granting security of tenure for business, professional and other tenants;[4] or

(2) Does not apply and so does not confer security of tenure, but only by virtue of an agreement to exclude that security entered into pursuant to Section 38A of the 1954 Act.[5]

These provisions are then complemented by the newly added Section 43(4) of the 1954 Act:

"This Part does not apply to a tenancy—

---

[1] The reason why Part 2 of the Code is specified here does not become immediately apparent until after one has read the transitional provisions, for which see Chapter Twelve. In essence, it is because Part 5 of the Code is capable of applying to some agreements entered into both under the Code and the Old Code.

[2] Sub-paragraph (4) is not considered here as it relates only to leases of land in Northern Ireland.

[3] Landlord and Tenant Act 1954.

[4] Communications Act 2003, Schedule 3A, Paragraph 29(2).

[5] Ibid, Paragraph 29(3).

(a) the primary purpose of which is to grant code rights within the meaning of Schedule 3A to the Communications Act 2003 (the electronic communications code), and

(b) which is granted after that Schedule comes into force."

The purpose of Paragraph 29 of the Code and Section 43(4) of the 1954 Act together is to prevent, when a code agreement in the form of a lease comes to an end, code operators from being able to choose between which regime they wish to renew their code rights under (the Code or Part 2 of the 1954 Act) – they will only have the benefit of one regime.[6] This was done to remedy an injustice that existed under the Old Code, by which code operators with 1954 Act-protected tenancies that conferred code rights could choose to renew under one or other of the schemes, depending on which was more advantageous to them in all the circumstances.

The Continuation of Code Rights

Pursuant to Paragraph 30(2) of the Code,[7] where a code right is binding on a person (the *"site provider"*) as the result of a code agreement, and under the terms of that code agreement either the code right ceases to be exercisable, the site provider ceases to be bound by it or, the site provider may bring the code agreement to an end so far as it relates to the code right in question:[8]

"the code agreement continues so that–

---

[6] And this purpose was given effect by the Supreme Court in *Cornerstone Telecommunications Infrastructure Ltd v Compton Beauchamp Estates Ltd* [2022] UKSC 18; [2022] 1 WLR 3360. See in particular [126]-[130] for a discussion as to the interrelationship between Parts 2, 4 and 5 of the Code by Lady Rose JSC (in the context of the identity of the *"occupier"* of the land),

[7] Which is contained in Part 5, and so does not apply the forms of lease specified in Paragraphs 29(2) to (4) of the Code.

[8] Communications Act 2003, Schedule 3A, Paragraph 30(1).

(a) the operator may continue to exercise that right, and

(b) the site provider continues to be bound by the right." [9]

Paragraph 30(2) of the Code is designed to prevent code agreements, and the code rights conferred thereunder, from being brought to an end by effluxion of time, or some other mechanism contained in the terms of the code agreement (in the case of a code agreement in the form of a lease, this could be by forfeiture).

Once a code right continues to be exercisable by the code operator solely by virtue of Paragraph 30(2) of the Code, only then does it become possible for site providers to seek to terminate the code right under Paragraph 31 of the Code (which is considered below), or for both site providers and code operators to seek to vary the terms of the code agreement under Paragraph 33 of the Code.[10]

It is important to note that, pursuant to Paragraph 30(3) of the Code, Paragraph 30(2) of the Code does not apply to interim or temporary code rights.

---

[9]   Ibid, Paragraph 30(2).

[10]   See ibid, Paragraphs 31(3)(b) and 33(3)(b). See Chapter Nine for variation of code agreements under Part 5.

The Termination of Code Agreements to Which Part 5 of the Code Applies

By the Site Provider

Pursuant to Paragraph 31 of the Code,[11] a site provider who is a party to a code agreement can give notice to the code operator to terminate the code agreement.[12]

A notice under Paragraph 30 of the Code must:

"(a) comply with paragraph 89 (notices given by persons other than operators),

(b) specify the date on which the site provider proposes the code agreement should come to an end, and

(c) state the ground on which the site provider proposes to bring the code agreement to an end." [13]

The requirements of Paragraph 89 of the Code are set out in Chapter Three.

Paragraph 31(3) provides that the date specified in the notice must fall:

---

[11] Which is contained in Part 5, and so does not apply the forms of lease specified in Paragraphs 29(2) to (4) of the Code.

[12] Ibid, Paragraph 31(1). But a site provider who is not party to the code agreement, as might arise when a concurrent lease is granted after grant of a code agreement, would not be entitled to serve such a notice: see *Vodafone Ltd v Gencomp (No. 7) Limited* [2022] UKUT 223 (LC), in particular at [121]. This has serious consequences for developers. Permission to appeal has been granted, so we will see in due course whether this potential threat crystallises.

[13] Ibid, Paragraph 31(2)

"(a) after the end of the period of 18 months beginning with the day on which the notice is given, and

(b) after the time at which, apart from paragraph 30, the code right to which the agreement relates would have ceased to be exercisable or to bind the site provider or at a time when, apart from that paragraph, the code agreement could have been brought to an end by the site provider." [14]

The interpretation of Paragraph 31(3) of the Code was central to *EE Ltd and Hutchison 3G UK Ltd v Edelwind Ltd and the Secretary of State for Housing, Communities and Local Government*.[15] The relevant facts are as follows:

(1) EE Ltd ("**EE**") acquired the right by a code agreement ("**Agreement 1**") under the Old Code to install and operate telecoms equipment on a rooftop site until 29 November 2024 from the Secretary of State for Housing, Communities and Local Government ("**S**"), the leaseholder of the site;

(2) At the same time, EE entered into an agreement ("**Agreement 2**") with both S and Edelwind Ltd ("**Edelwind**"), the freeholder of the site, in which Edelwind agreed to be bound by the terms of Agreement 1;

(3) In 2010, EE sought to assign Agreements 1 and 2 to itself and Hutchison 3G UK Ltd ("**H3G**"), another code operator;

(4) On 14 December 2018, Edelwind exercised a break clause in its lease with S, which would bring S's lease of the site to an end on 2 April 2021

(5) In December 2019, S and Edelwind served notices on both EE and H3G under Paragraph 31 of the Code, seeking to end the agreement

---

[14] Ibid, Paragraph 31(3).

[15] [2020] 9 WLUK 223.

conferring code rights (without specific reference to either Agreement 1 or Agreement 2) on dates after 21 April 2021; and

(5) EE and H3G challenged the validity of the notices given under Paragraph 31 of the Code, as they claimed that, *inter alia*, neither S nor Edelwind could serve any notice under Paragraph 31 of the Code until after 29 November 2024.

The Tribunal found that, by virtue of the fact that S's lease would come to an end on 2 April 2021 by virtue of Edelwind's exercise of its break clause, Agreement 1 would similarly come to an end on 2 April 2021 and thereafter continue under Paragraph 30(2) of the Code.[16] As the terms of Agreement 2 merely provided that Edelwind be bound by the terms of Agreement 1, Agreement 2 would similarly come to an end on 2 April 2021 and continue in the same vein thereafter.[17]

Paragraph 31(3) does not require that any notice given thereunder be given on a date after the relevant code agreement has begun to continue by virtue of Paragraph 30(2) of the Code. It only requires that eighteen months' notice be given, and the termination date be a date after the relevant code agreement has begun to continue by virtue of Paragraph 30(2) of the Code. As a result, the notices given to EE were valid.[18] As these proceedings concerned the validity of the notices, the Tribunal did not determine whether any of the relevant grounds were made out.

The four potential grounds set out in Paragraph 31(4) are:

"(a) that the code agreement ought to come to an end as a result of substantial breaches by the operator of its obligations under the agreement;

---

[16] Ibid, at [38].

[17] Ibid, at [49].

[18] The notices given to H3G were not effective, as the Tribunal determined that EE's attempt to assign each Agreements 1 and 2 to itself and H3G in 2010 were ineffective.

(b) that the code agreement ought to come to an end because of persistent delays by the operator in making payments to the site provider under the agreement;

(c) that the site provider intends to redevelop all or part of the land to which the code agreement relates, or any neighbouring land, and could not reasonably do so unless the code agreement comes to an end;

(d) that the operator is not entitled to the code agreement because the test under paragraph 21 for the imposition of the agreement on the site provider is not met."[19]

The first two grounds relate to breach of the terms of the code agreement; the site provider should not be compelled to remain party to a contract that the code operator does not honour. The second two grounds replicate both the redevelopment defence and the general test for the imposition of a code agreement present in Paragraph 21 of the Code.[20]

Following service of a notice under Paragraph 31 of the Code, Paragraph 32 provides for what happens next. The code agreement will come to an end on the date stated in the notice, unless the code operator either:

"(a) within the period of three months beginning with the day on which the notice is given... gives the site provider a counter-notice in accordance with sub-paragraph (3), and

(b) within the period of three months beginning with the day on which the counter-notice is given, the operator applies to the court for an order under paragraph 34."[21]

---

[19] Ibid, Paragraph 31(4).

[20] For which see Chapter Four.

[21] Communications Act 2003, Schedule 3A, Paragraph 32(1).

Together with complying with Paragraph 88 of the Code,[22] the counter-notice must state:

"(a) that the operator does not want the existing code agreement to come to an end,

(b) that the operator wants the site provider to agree to confer or be otherwise bound by the existing code right on new terms, or

(c) that the code operator wants the site provider to agree to confer or be otherwise bound by a new code right in place of the existing code right."[23]

Whereas Sub-paragraph 32(3)(a) of the Code allows the code operator to simply oppose an attempt by the site provider to terminate the existing code agreement, Sub-paragraphs 32(3)(b) and (c) of the Code allow the code operator to instead seek to vary their existing contractual relationship by way of its counter-notice, instead of having to serve a separate notice under Paragraph 33 of the Code. The parties' ability to seek variation of code agreements is considered in Chapter Nine.

Importantly, the time limits and consequences set out in Paragraph 32(1) of the Code do not apply in the event that the code operator and site provider agree to the continuation of the extant code agreement.[24]

Where no agreement is reached between the parties, and the code operator serves its counter-notice and then applies under Paragraph 34 of the Code:

"(4) If… the court decides that the site provider has established any of the grounds stated in the site provider's notice under paragraph 31, the court must order that the code agreement comes to an end in accordance with the order.

---

[22] For which see Chapter Three.

[23] Communications Act 2003, Schedule 3A, Paragraph 32(3).

[24] Ibid, Paragraph 32(2).

(5) Otherwise the court must make one of the orders specified in paragraph 34." [25]

In the event that the site provider fails to make out one of the grounds contained in its notice, and the code operator's counter-notice relied upon Paragraph 32(3)(a) of the Code (stating that it does not want the existing code agreement to come to an end), the Tribunal will most likely make an order pursuant to Paragraph 34(2) of the Code:

"that the operator may continue to exercise the existing code right in accordance with the existing code agreement for such period as may be specified in the order (so that the code agreement has effect accordingly)."

Other potential orders that can be made under Paragraph 34 of the Code (including where the counter-notice relies upon Paragraph 32(3)(b) or (c) of the Code) are considered in Chapter Nine.

It should be noted that, whilst these provisions are yet to be in force, Section 69 of the Product Security and Telecommunications Infrastructure Act 2022 makes amendments to Paragraph 32 (effect of notice to terminate an agreement) and Paragraph 33 (modifying the terms of an expired agreement) of the Code by introduction of a new paragraph (3A) which provides that the counter-notice must contain information about the availability of ADR and the consequences of refusal of ADR. Further the operator is to be required to consider ADR if it is reasonably practicable to do so before making an order by a new sub-paragraph (5) and providing for notice to be given by either the operator or the relevant person that they wish to engage in ADR.

Further, Section 69(5) of PSTIA will amend the Code to empower the Tribunal to award costs in relation to any unreasonable refusal by a party to engage in ADR.

---

[25] Ibid, Paragraph 32(4) and (5).

<u>By the Code Operator</u>

Curiously, Paragraph 31(1) of the Code provides only that site providers can serve notices on code operators seeking to bring code agreements to an end; not the other way around. In fact, the Code does not provide any express machinery through which a code operator can seek to terminate a code agreement to which Part 5 of the Code applies (other than in the context of a novation under Paragraph 33 of the Code).[26]

Given that Paragraph 30(1) of the Code provides that a code agreement will continue in any circumstances where a code right ceases to be exercisable under the code agreement, it likely follows that a break clause (or other contractually-provided means of termination) exercised by a code operator will not be effective to terminate the code agreement.

As set out in Chapter Two, Paragraph 3 of the Code provides that a *"code right"* is *"a right for the statutory purposes"* set out therein. It is therefore conceivable that if, by the effective date of a break notice given by a code operator under a code agreement, the code operator has vacated the site, removed its telecoms apparatus, and so no longer exercises its code right for any of the statutory purposes set out in Paragraph 3 of the Code, then the code agreement will not continue under Paragraph 30(1) of the Code because the relevant right is no longer a code right, and Paragraph 30(1) of the Code only takes effect to continue code agreements that confer code rights.

Under those circumstances it might be possible for a code operator to effectively terminate a code agreement by giving notice. However, unless and until there is a reported case on this issue, whether or not a code operator is capable of effectively terminating a code agreement (in the circumstances set out above, or any others that may operate similarly) remains uncertain.

---

[26] For which, see Chapter Nine.

By Consent

A similar issue arises in the context of whether a code operator and site provider can agree to a surrender of a code agreement to which Part 5 of the Code applies by consent that avoids Paragraph 30(2) of the Code taking effect to continue the code agreement.

Paragraph 30(1)(b) of the Code provides that the code agreement will continue where the code right ceases to be exercisable, the site provider ceases to be bound by it or, the site provider may bring the code agreement to an end so far as it relates to the code right in question *"under the terms of the agreement"*.

In theory, a surrender of a code agreement that is not achieved pursuant to exercise of contractual terms set out in the code agreement itself does not take effect *"under the terms of the* [code] *agreement"* in question.

Again, whether or not such a surrender would be effective to terminate a code agreement remains uncertain pending authority on the subject.

Summary

In summary:

(1) Part 5 of the Code, which covers continuation, termination and modification of code agreements applies to all agreements falling under Part 2 of the Code, except where the code agreement is a lease and the primary purpose of the lease is not to grant code rights, or is one to which the 1954 Act applies (or which does not apply because of an agreement to exclude that security as provided under Section 38A of the 1954 Act);

(2) Code agreements to which Part 5 of the code applies will continue under Paragraph 30(2) of the Code, notwithstanding that the terms of the code agreement may provide for their earlier termination;

(3) Site providers can seek to terminate code agreements to which Part 5 of the Code applies on a date after the code agreement has begun to continue under Paragraph 30(2) of the Code by giving eighteen months' notice to the code operator and relying on one of four grounds. The code agreement will then terminate unless the code operator gives a counter- notice and subsequently applies to the Tribunal for either an order that the code agreement continue on the same terms, or be varied. The Tribunal will terminate the code agreement if one of the grounds is made out. If not, the Tribunal may make other orders under Paragraph 34 of the Code;

(4) It is conceivable, but not certain, that a code operator can exercise a break clause in a code agreement to which Part 5 of the Code applies, in order to terminate a code agreement and evade Paragraph 30(2) of the Code, provided that it has ceased to use the code right for one of the statutory purposes set out in Paragraph 3 of the Code by the date specified in the break notice; and

(5) It is conceivable, but not certain, that the site provider and code operator can terminate a code agreement to which Part 5 of the Code applies by consent by effective a surrender, provided that surrender is not achieved pursuant to terms set out in the code agreement.

CHAPTER NINE

VARIATION OF CODE AGREEMENTS, AND INTERIM PAYMENTS OF CONSIDERATION

In this chapter we address:

(1) The procedure for variation of code agreements to which Part 5 of the Code applies;

(2) The orders that can be made by the Tribunal in an application to modify a code agreement under Part 5 of the Code; and

(3) Interim payments of consideration pending applications to terminate or vary code agreements under Part 5 of the Code.

The Procedure for Varying the Terms of a Code Agreement

By the Code Operator's Counter-Notice under Paragraph 32(3)(b) or (c)

As set out in Chapter Eight, a code operator may respond to a termination notice given to it by the *"site provider"* under Paragraph 33 of the Code by with a counter-notice under Paragraph 32.

The code operator may respond under Sub-paragraph 32(3)(a) of the Code, stating that it does not want the code agreement to come to an end, or the code operator can state under Sub-paragraph 32(3)(b) or (c) that it either wants the site provider to agree to confer or be otherwise bound by:

(1) The existing code right on new terms;[1] or

(2) A new code right in place of the existing code right.[2]

Pursuant to Paragraph 32(5) of the Code, if the site provider is unable to make out any of the grounds contained in its termination notice *"the court must make one of the orders specified in paragraph 34"*, which are considered in more detail below.

<u>By Either Party under Paragraph 33</u>

The procedure for a change to the terms of a code agreement, to which Part 5 of the Code applies, that either of the parties to the code agreement (that is both the site provider and operator) may utilise is set out at Paragraph 33 of the Code. Either party may, by notice that complies with the provisions of Paragraph 33(1), require the other party to agree that that:

"(a) the code agreement should have effect with modified terms,

(b) where under the code agreement more than one code right is conferred by or otherwise binds the site provider, that the agreement should no longer provide for an existing code right to be conferred by or otherwise bind the site provider,

(c) the code agreement should—

(i) confer an additional code right on the operator, or

(ii) provide that the site provider is otherwise bound by an additional code right, or

(d) the existing code agreement should be terminated and a new agreement should have effect between the parties which—

---

[1] Communications Act 2003, Schedule 3A, Paragraph 32(3)(a).

[2] Ibid, Paragraph 32(3)(b).

(i) confers a code right on the operator, or

(ii) provides for a code right to bind the site provider."

Paragraph 33(2)(a) of the Code provides that any notice given under Paragraph 33(1) must comply with either Paragraph 88 or 89 of the Code, depending on whether the notice is given by the operator or site provider.[3] Further, pursuant to Paragraph 33(2)(b), the notice must specify:

"(i) the day from which it is proposed the modified terms should have effect,

(ii) the day from which the agreement should no longer provide for the code right to be conferred by or bind the site provider,

(iii) the day from which it is proposed that the additional code right should be conferred by or otherwise bind the site provider, or

(iv) the day on which it is proposed the existing code agreement should be terminated and from which the new agreement should have effect,

(as the case may be)"

Paragraph 33(2)(c) of the Code contains further requirements for the notice to set out the details of:

"(i) the proposed modified terms,

(ii) the code right it is proposed should no longer be conferred by or otherwise bind the site provider,

(iii) the proposed additional code right, or

(iv) the proposed terms of the agreement,

(as the case may be)."

---

3   For which, see Chapter Three.

Similar to termination notices, Paragraph 33(3) of the Code provides that the day specified in accordance with Paragraph 33(2)(b) must be:

(1) After the end of six months starting from the date the notice is given (twelve months shorter than for termination notices); and

(2) On a date after the code agreement has begun to continue under Paragraph 30(2) of the Code.[4]

Paragraph 33(4) and (5) of the Code provide that, in the event that agreement on the proposal in the notice is not reached within six months commencing on the day the notice is given, either party may apply for an order under Paragraph 34.[5]

The Orders the Tribunal May Make

Paragraph 34 of the Code specifies the orders that the Tribunal may make on an application under Paragraph 32(1)(b) or Paragraph 33(5) of the Code. The powers conferred on the Tribunal are broad.

The powers include, by Paragraph 34(2) of the Code, continuation of the existing right in accordance with the existing agreement for a period specified in the order. This is likely to be used either where a site provider has failed to make out any of the grounds contained in its termination notice, or on an application to vary the terms of the code agreement where neither party is able to persuade the Tribunal to make any of the other available orders.

The Tribunal may modify the terms relating to the existing code right under Paragraph 34(3) of the Code. If more than one code right is conferred under the agreement, Paragraph 34(4) of the Code empowers the Tribunal to modify the code agreement so that it no longer provides

---

4   For which, see Chapter Eight.

5   It does not appear that it is only the person that gave the notice that may apply. The wording of Paragraph 33(4) is wide enough to permit either the party who serves or receives the notice to make the application to the Tribunal.

for one or more code rights to bind the site provider (provided at least one code right in the original code agreement remains conferred or binding thereunder). Further, by Paragraph 34(5) of the Code, the Tribunal may modify the agreement to confer an additional code right on the operator, or to provide that the site provider is otherwise bound by an additional code right.

Paragraph 34(6) of the Code empowers the Tribunal to vary the code agreement by novation:

"The court may order the termination of the code agreement relating to the existing right and order the operator and the site provider to enter into a new agreement which–

(a) confers a code right on the operator, or

(b) provides for a code right to bind the site provider."

The existing code agreement will continue until the new agreement takes effect,[6] and the Code applies to the new agreement as if it were an agreement under Part 2 of the Code.[7]

Paragraph 34(9) of the Code provides that the terms providing for the new code right are to be agreed between the operator and site provider. If terms cannot be agreed, either party may apply to the Tribunal which will then impose those terms,[8] and in such a case the Tribunal is also required to have regard to the terms of the existing code agreement.[9]

Paragraph 34(11) of the Code provides that Paragraphs 23(2) to (8) (which relate to the terms of an agreement),[10] Paragraph 24 (how

---

[6]   Communications Act 2003, Schedule 3A, Paragraph 34(7).

[7]   Ibid, Paragraph 34(8).

[8]   Ibid, Paragraph 34(10).

[9]   Ibid, Paragraph 34(12).

[10]   For which, see Chapter Five.

consideration is to be determined),[11] Paragraph 25 (rights to the payment of compensation) and Paragraph 84 (compensation under the Code) [12] apply to an order under Sub-paragraphs (3), (4) and (5) so far as it modifies or specifies the terms of the agreement, and to an order under Sub-paragraph (1), just as they apply to an order under Paragraph 20 of the Code.

Paragraph 34(13) of the Code requires the Tribunal to have regard to all the circumstances of the case in deciding what order to make. Certain circumstances are specified as being matters which must, in particular be considered. These matters are:

"(a) the operator's business and technical needs,

(b) the use that the site provider is making of the land to which the existing code agreement relates,

(c) any duties imposed on the site provider by an enactment, and

(d) the amount of consideration payable by the operator to the site provider under the existing code agreement."

Where an order is made pursuant to Paragraph 34 of the Code, the Tribunal has power under Paragraph 34(14) to direct the code operator to pay the site provider the amount (if any) by which A exceeds B in which:

"(a) A is the amount of consideration that would have been payable by the operator to the site provider for the relevant period if that amount had been assessed on the same basis as the consideration payable as the result of the order, and

(b) B is the amount of consideration payable by the operator to the site provider for the relevant period."

---

[11] See Chapter Six.

[12] See Chapter Seven.

And the *"relevant period"* for the purpose of Paragraph 34(14) of the Code is defined in Paragraph 34(15) as the period (if any) that:

"(a) begins on the date on which, apart from the operation of paragraph 30, the code right to which the existing code agreement relates would have ceased to be exercisable or to bind the site provider or from which, apart from that paragraph, the code agreement could have been brought to an end by the site provider, and

(b) ends on the date on which the order is made."

The exercise of Tribunal's powers to make orders under Paragraph 34 was considered as a preliminary issue by the President of the Tribunal, Mr Justice Fancourt, in *EE Ltd and Hutchison 3G UK Ltd v Stephenson and AP Wireless II (UK) Ltd*.[13] In that case, following the expiry of a lease that was a subsisting agreement to which Part 5 of the Code applied,[14] the code operator served the site provider with a notice under Paragraph 33(1)(d) of the Code seeking that the parties enter into a new agreement to confer a code right at a considerably lower rent.

The parties were unable to reach agreement within six months, so the code operator applied under Paragraph 33(5) of the Code for an order under Paragraph 34(6). The site provider opposed the application on the basis that, when having regard to all the circumstances of the case and the factors contained at Paragraph 34(13) of the Code, the Tribunal should not make an order under Paragraph 34(6) because the code operator had failed to advance a site-specific need for a novation of the existing agreement. This argument was advanced reliant in part on the principle in *O'May v City of London Real Property Co Ltd*,[15] which provides that in lease renewals under Part 2 of the 1954 Act there is a presumption against change of the terms of the existing agreement, and so a heavy onus lay on the party seeking variation to justify it.

---

[13] [2021] UKUT 167 (LC).

[14] For which, see Chapter Twelve.

[15] [1983] 2 AC 726.

The President initially observed at [46] that *"The Code was intended to confer broader rights and more flexibility on operators, in view of the impending arrival of 5G networks and new technology."* He went on at [47] to explain that whilst Parliament had indeed decided that the Code should not have retrospective effect. *"It cannot have been intended that the public benefits and investments incentives conferred by the new Code would be stultified by the continuation of subsisting agreements, with more limited rights at higher rents or fees, for a significant time after their expiry dates."*

In this context, the President concluded that *"it seems clear that an operator under a subsisting agreement should not have to prove a site-specific justification for the replacement of an expired subsisting agreement with a new Code-compliant agreement. The significant additional rights conferred by the Code, the benefit of some or all of which will have been denied the operator for the duration of the subsisting agreement, are themselves a reason for the grant of a new agreement on different terms."*[16]

The President then considered what it should mean for the Tribunal to have regard to the *"business and technical needs"* of the code operator under Paragraph 34(13)(a) of the Code, and found at [51] that:

"Parliament cannot have intended to impose on an operator a requirement to prove a specific need for the particular order sought in relation to the site in issue. The business and technical needs of an operator are its reasonable requirements as regards the statutory purposes, namely the provision of its network and an infrastructure system. It seems to me that they may also include a need to have a standard form of agreement for its code agreements, for estate management reasons."[17]

---

[16] It follows that the President's reasoning against a site-specific need for renewal is limited in scope to where agreements entered into under the Old Code are being renewed under the Code. We may see this argument re-surface in the future where a code operator seeks a novation on new terms of an agreement entered into under the Code, and may see a different conclusion reached.

[17] Agreeing with the decision of the Court of Session (Inner House) in *EE Ltd and Hutchinson 3G UK Ltd v Duncan* [2021] CSIH 27.

The President held that whilst there were indeed similarities in the wording of Paragraph 34(14) of the Code and Section 35 of the 1954 Act, the provisions were not the same and the purpose underlying the 1954 Act *"was very different"* from the purpose underlying the Code.[18] Instead, *"site providers are required to put up with a degree of change in the public interest of facilitating the provision of a choice of high quality networks."*[19] It followed that the case law under Section 35 of the 1954 Act, including the principle in *O'May*, do not directly apply to orders under Paragraph 34 of the Code. [20]

A second issue arose because the code operator had, in its application under Paragraph 33(5) following service of the notice under Paragraph 33(1)(d) of the Code, sought in the alternative that the Tribunal make a different order under Paragraph 34 of the Code. The site provider argued that this was not permitted, as it was an application for an order varying the extant code agreement that had not been the subject of a prior notice seeking said change.

The President agreed with the site provider and struck out the code operator's application for an alternative order: *"if the notice proposed termination and a new agreement on terms annexed, the giver of the notice cannot apply to the court for modification of the existing agreement on different terms..."*[21] *"it is not permissible for an applicant to plead an alternative case for a different change to the existing agreement unless it has served a notice that identifies the relief sought."*[22]

However, the Tribunal went on to explain that it would have been open to the site provider to *"waive any non-compliance if they are content to*

---

[18] [2021] UKUT 167 (LC) at [53].

[19] Ibid, at [55].

[20] See also *On Tower UK Ltd v JH & FW Green Ltd* [2022] 4 WLR 27 at [47]-[49], where this argument similarly got little-to-no traction.

[21] Ibid, at [63].

[22] Ibid, at [66].

engage with the application that has been made" [23] or *"to plead that an order terminating the existing agreement and for a new agreement should not be made because, in the particular circumstances of the case, a different order that the court may make is more appropriate, or is sufficient for the applicant's needs."* [24]

The Tribunal has recently discovered a potential lacuna in the machinery of Part 5 of the Code in niche circumstances, as it set out in *Vodafone Ltd v Gencomp (No. 7) Limited.* [25] The facts of that case were as follows:

(1) Vodafone was granted a lease of parts of a building by its old freeholder, under the Old Code;

(2) Gencomp was the new freeholder. In 2018, before expiry of Vodafone's lease but after the Code came into effect, It granted a concurrent lease to AP Wireless II (UK) Ltd ("**APW**");

(3) APW became Vodafone's immediate landlord, Gencomp no longer having an immediate right to possession;

(4) Vodafone carefully served various forms of both Paragraph 20 and 33 notices on each Gencomp and APW, covering its bases to assure it could acquire new rights from one of them; and

(5) Vodafone said that only Gencomp could grant the rights, and APW should be bound by them. APW thought the opposite.

The Upper Tribunal held that neither Gencomp nor APW could grant Vodafone new rights pursuant to its Part 33 notice(s). This was because:

---

23 Ibid, at [63].

24 Ibid, at [65].

25 [2022] UKUT 223 (LC). Permission to appeal has been granted.

(1)   Under Paragraph 33 of the Code, only a *"site provider who Is party to a code agreement"* can be compelled to grant new code rights; and

(2)   Under Paragraph 9 of the Code, only the *"occupier"* can grant code rights.

It follows that a new code agreement can only be imposed under Paragraph 34 of the code if a person is both a *"site provider who is party to a code agreement"* and the *"occupier"*.

Unfortunately, whereas Gencomp was a site provider and a party to the code agreement (unlike APW),[26] following the Supreme Court's decision in *Cornerstone Telecommunications Infrastructure Ltd v Compton Beauchamp Estates Ltd* [27] it was APW that was the relevant *"occupier"*.[28]

The Upper Tribunal went on to rule that the reference could continue under Part 4 of the Code pursuant to the Paragraph 20 Notice served by Vodafone on APW, so Vodafone was not without an avenue by which It could acquire code rights.

Interim Payments of Consideration

Where there is a pending application by either the code operator or site provider under Paragraph 32(1)(b) or 33(5) of the Code,[29] Paragraph 35 of the Code gives the site provider three options as to how consideration payable under the extant code agreement should be treated in the interim. The site provider may:

---

[26]   Ibid, [100]-[104].

[27]   [2022] 1 WLR 3360.

[28]   [2022] UKUT 223 (LC), [94]-[96].

[29]   Communications Act 2003, Schedule 3A, Paragraph 35(1).

(1) Agree with the code operator that they will continue to receive the payments of consideration to which they are entitled under the extant code agreement, until the relevant application has been determined;[30]

(2) Agree with the code operator that it will pay to the site provider different payments of consideration to which they are entitled under the extant code agreement, until the relevant application has been determined;[31] or

(3) Apply to the Tribunal for it to determine what consideration should be payable to the site provider under the extant code agreement until the application has been determined.[32]

In the event that the Tribunal is required to determine the consideration to be paid, it will do so in accordance with the basis set out in Paragraph 24 of the Code.[33] This scheme clearly draws inspiration from applications for interim rent under Section 24A of the 1954 Act.

Amendments Under PSTIA

By Section 68 of the Product Security and Telecommunications Act 2022 ("**PSTIA**"), which is also not in force at the time of publication, amendments are made to Paragraph 25 of the Code in respect of arrangements pending determination of an application under Paragraph 32 or 33. This is, primarily, by the insertion of further sub-paragraphs to Paragraph 35 although there are other amendments to Paragraph 35. The key additions are as follows:

"(2A) The operator or the site provider may apply to the court for—

---

[30] Ibid, Paragraph 35(2)(a).

[31] Ibid, Paragraph 35(2)(b).

[32] Ibid, Paragraph 35(2)(c).

[33] Ibid, Paragraph 35(3).

(a) an order specifying the payments of consideration to be made by the operator to the site provider under the agreement relating to the existing code right until the application for an order under paragraph 32(1)(b) or 33(5) has been finally determined;

(b) an order otherwise modifying the terms of that agreement until that time.

(2B) An order under sub-paragraph (2A)(a) may provide for the order to have effect from the date of the application for the order...

(4) In determining whether to make an order under sub-paragraph (2A)(b), the court must have regard to all the circumstances of the case, and in particular to—

(a) the terms of the agreement relating to the existing code right,

(b) the operator's business and technical needs,

(c) the use that the site provider is making of the land to which the agreement relates,

(d) any duties imposed on the site provider by an enactment, and

(e) the amount of consideration payable by the operator to the site provider under the agreement."

Summary

In summary:

(1) Where a site provider gives a code operator a termination notice, the code operator's counter-notice may seek variation of the code agreement (in the event that the site provider is unable to make out any of the grounds for termination);

(2) Alternatively, either party may serve a notice requiring the other to agree that the code agreement be modified, which can include modification of terms, the removal of rights, the inclusion of

additional rights, or a new agreement conferring one or more new code rights;

(3) The notice must comply with the formalities required under Paragraphs 88 or 89 of the Code (as applicable), and must specify the date (no less than six months from the date of the notice, and after the date on which the code agreement began to continue under Paragraph 30(2) of the Code) on which the modified terms, additional or removed code rights, or new agreement shall have effect, and adequate details of the changes;

(4) In the event of no agreement within 6 months of the date notice is given, either party may apply for an order under Paragraph 34 of the Code;

(5) The powers of the Tribunal under the Code are wide ranging and include powers to continue the existing agreement, modify its terms, remove or add code rights, or order that a new agreement conferring new code rights be entered into;

(6) In making an order, the Tribunal is required to consider all the circumstances, but to have particular regard to four factors set out in Paragraph 34(13). There is not the same presumption against change which applies to renewal under the 1954 Act;

(7) A code operator need not provide a site-specific justification for a variation of the terms of the code agreement;

(8) The provisions relating to consideration and compensation in other Parts of the Code apply to such an order;

(9) The Tribunal has power to direct the operator to pay the site provider an amount of consideration by reference to the formula set out in Paragraph 34(14) of the Code;

(10) When an application is pending in the Tribunal either for termination or variation of a code agreement, the parties to the code

agreement can agree to maintain the same consideration payments, agree to vary them, or require the Tribunal to determine what the consideration payments up until determination of the pending application should have been, in a similar fashion to how interim rent applications under the 1954 Act operate; and

(11) In the near future, interim rent machinery amendments under PSTIA will come into force.

CHAPTER TEN

REMOVAL OF APPARATUS

In this chapter we consider the removal of apparatus as provided for in Part 6 of the Code, including:

(1) The means by which a person can discover whether apparatus is on land pursuant to a code right;

(2) The cases in which a landowner has the right to require the removal of electronic communications apparatus or the restoration of land;

(3) The cases in which a landowner or occupier of neighbouring land has the right to require removal of apparatus; and

(4) The means by which a right to require removal of apparatus or restoration of land can be enforced.

The Procedure for Determining Whether Apparatus is on Land Pursuant to a Code Right

Paragraph 39 of the Code enables a landowner or occupier to ascertain whether apparatus is on land pursuant to a code right. The process enables the landowner to serve a notice requiring a code operator to disclose whether:

"(a) the operator owns electronic communications apparatus on, under or over land in which the landowner has an interest or uses such apparatus for the purposes of the operator's network, or

(b) the operator has the benefit of a code right entitling the operator to keep electronic communications apparatus on, under or over land in which the landowner has an interest." [1]

Further rights are conferred by Paragraph 39(2) of the Code, where the landowner or occupier of neighbouring land may by notice require the code operator to disclose whether it owns apparatus over land that forms, or but for the apparatus would form, a means of access to the neighbouring land, or uses such apparatus for the purpose of the operator's network, or has a code right entitling it to keep such apparatus on, over or under such land.

Pursuant to Paragraph 39(3) of the Code, any of these notices served must comply with the requirements of Paragraph 89. [2]

By Paragraph 39(5) the code operator must bear the costs of any action taken by the landowner or occupier under Paragraph 40 to enforce the removal of the apparatus providing the conditions in Sub-paragraph (4) are met, namely:

"(a) the operator does not, before the end of the period of three months beginning with the date on which the notice under sub-paragraph (1) or (2) was given, give a notice to the landowner or occupier that—

(i) complies with paragraph 88 (notices given by operators), and

(ii) discloses the information sought by the landowner or occupier,

(b) the landowner or occupier takes action under paragraph 40 to enforce the removal of the apparatus, and

(c) it is subsequently established that—

---

[1]   Communications Act 2003, Schedule 3A, Paragraph 39(1).

[2]   For which, see Chapter Three.

(i) the operator owns the apparatus or uses it for the purposes of the operator's network, and

(ii) the operator has the benefit of a code right entitling the operator to keep the apparatus on, under or over the land."

The Conditions Required for a Landowner to have the Right to Require Removal of Apparatus

Paragraph 37(1) of the Code explains that a landowner has the right to require the removal of telecoms apparatus *"if and only if"* one or more of certain conditions are met. It follows that if none of the specified conditions is met there is no right to require the operator to remove the equipment.

The First Condition

The first condition is set out in Paragraph 37(2) of the Code. This is that the landowner has never since the coming into force of the Code been bound by a code right entitling the code operator to keep apparatus on, under or over the land. This is self-explanatory.

However, this condition is subject to Paragraph 37(4) considered below.

The Second Condition

The second condition is contained in Paragraph 37(3) of the Code. That is that a code right entitling the operator to keep apparatus on, under or over land has come to an end or ceased to bind the landowner in any one of the following four situations:

(1) Pursuant to Paragraph 37(3)(a) of the Code, where interim code rights have expired as provided for at Paragraph 26(7) and (8) of the Code;[3]

---

[3]   For which, see Chapter Four.

(2) Pursuant to Paragraph 37(3)(b) of the Code, where code rights have been terminated under Paragraph 32(1);[4]

(3) Pursuant to Paragraph 37(3)(c) of the Code, where code rights have been terminated by order under Paragraph 32(4),[5] 34(4) or 34(6);[6] and

(4) Pursuant to Paragraph 37(3)(d) of the Code, where *"the right was granted by a lease to which Part 5 of this code does not apply"*[7] and the lease has ceased to bind the landowner.

<u>Excluding Qualification Under the First or Second Conditions</u>

All of the situations specified in each the first condition under Paragraph 37(2) and the second condition as provided in Paragraph 37(3)(a) to (d) are subject to Paragraph 37(4) of the Code. This provides:

"(4) The landowner does not meet the first or second condition if—

(a) the land is occupied by a person who—

(i) conferred a code right (which is in force) entitling an operator to keep the apparatus on, under or over the land, or

(ii) is otherwise bound by such a right, and

(b) that code right was not conferred in breach of a covenant enforceable by the landowner."

---

4   For which, see Chapter Eight.

5   For which, see Chapter Eight.

6   For which, see Chapter Nine.

7   For which, see Chapter Eight.

The Third Condition

The third condition is set out at Paragraph 37(6) of the Code. It addresses the situation where the apparatus is not or is longer required for use within the network. There are three criteria:

"(a) an operator has the benefit of a code right entitling the operator to keep the apparatus on, under or over the land, but

(b) the apparatus is not, or is no longer, used for the purposes of the operator's network, and

(c) there is no reasonable likelihood that the apparatus will be used for that purpose."

The Fourth Condition

The fourth condition is provided in Paragraph 37(7) of the Code and is directed towards the status of the code operator. It contains three elements:

"(a) this code has ceased to apply to a person so that the person is no longer entitled under this code to keep the apparatus on, under or over the land,

(b) the retention of the apparatus on, under or over the land is not authorised by a scheme contained in an order under section 117, and

(c) there is no other person with a right conferred by or under this code to keep the apparatus on, under or over the land."

The Fifth Condition

The fifth condition is that the apparatus was kept on the land pursuant to a transport right under Part 7 of the Code or a street work right pursuant to Part 8 of the Code, and that right has ceased to be exercisable pursuant to Paragraph 54(9) of the Code (Paragraph 54 of the Code addresses the position if land ceases to be transport land) and there is no other person with a code right to keep the apparatus on, over or under the land.[8]

The Circumstances in which a Landowner or Occupier of Neighbouring Land has the Right to Require Removal of Apparatus

There are two conditions which must be met for a landowner or occupier of any land (described as *"neighbouring land"*) to require the removal of apparatus. The first is set out in Paragraph 38(2) of the Code, namely that the apparatus *"interferes with or obstructs a means of access to or from the neighbouring land."* By Paragraph 38(3) of the Code, the second condition is that the landowner or occupier of the neighbouring land is not bound by a code right pursuant to Paragraph 3(h) of the Code, which entitles the operator to cause the interference or obstruction.

However, Paragraph 38(4) provides that the landowner of the neighbouring land, who is not the occupier of the land, does not meet the second condition if the land is occupied by a person who conferred a code right which is in force and which entitles the operator to cause the interference or obstruction, or is otherwise bound by such a right unless the code right was conferred in breach of a covenant enforceable by the landowner.

The key case concerning removal of apparatus is *Evolution (Shinfield) LLP and Others v British Telecommunications PLC*.[9] The facts of this case were as follows:

(1) Evolution (Shinfield) LLP (**"Evolution"**), a property developer, owned a large development site immediately west of a roundabout;

---

8   These provisions fall outside the scope of this book.

9   [2019] UKUT 127 (LC).

(2) In 2011, the code operator had installed a telecoms cabinet on a footway on the roundabout;

(3) In 2012, Evolution obtained planning consent for a major new housing development which included creating a new exit from the roundabout. That exit was to go straight through the footway where the cabinet was situated. It was not possible to redesign the roundabout to avoid the removal of the cabinet;

(4) C sought an order under Paragraph 40 of the Code for the removal of the cabinet, and the specification of works for said relocation came to nearly £300,000.00; and

(5) The reference to the Tribunal was a dispute regarding who was responsible for paying for the works, but the preliminary issue arose as to whether Evolution could even require the removal.

Evolution relied on the right conferred by Paragraph 38 of the Code, but the code operator argued that this applied only to means of access that were in existence at the time of the installation of the apparatus. Martin Rodger QC dismissed the reference, and held that *"interferes with or obstructs a means of access to or from neighbouring land"* at Paragraph 38 of the Code refers to *"an existing means of access, rather than something potential."* Importantly, the means of access had to be extant at the time the code rights were conferred.

The Tribunal considered that this is consistent with the general scheme of the Code, in particular the circumstances (set out in Paragraph 13(2) of the Code) under which a code operator is permitted to interfere with or obstruct means of access to neighbouring land. The Tribunal considered that Paragraph 38 of the Code was simply the corollary of Paragraph 13 of the Code; Paragraph 38 of the Code is merely the means of enforcing that rights of way that were in place when the apparatus was installed may not be interfered with unless the owner of the right of way is bound by them.

The Procedure for Removal of Apparatus by the Landowner or Occupier

Pursuant to Paragraph 40(1) of the Code, removal of apparatus by the landowner or occupier pursuant to Paragraph 37 and 38 of the Code is exercisable only in accordance with Paragraph 40 of the Code.

The Notice

Removal is triggered by service of a notice by the landowner or occupier pursuant to Paragraph 40(2) of the Code requiring the operator to remove the apparatus and restore the land to the condition it was in prior to the apparatus being situated on, over or under the land. Pursuant to Paragraphs 40(3)(b) and (4) of the Code, the notice must comply with Paragraph 89 of the Code [10] and specify the period within which the operator must complex the works which must be reasonable.

The Position if No Agreement is Reached

If agreement is not reached within twenty-eight days beginning on the date notice was given in relation to the matters listed in Paragraph 40(5) of the Code then, by Paragraph 40(6) of the Code, the landowner or occupier may apply to the Tribunal either for an order under Paragraph 44(1) of the Code (which requires the operator to remove the apparatus) or for an order under Paragraph 44(3) of the Code (enabling the landowner to sell the apparatus).

The matters listed in Paragraph 40(5) about what agreement must be reached in order to avoid the landowner or occupier having the right to apply to the Tribunal are:

"(a) that the operator will remove the apparatus;

(b) that the operator will restore the land to its condition before the apparatus was placed on, under or over the land;

---

[10] For which, see Chapter Three.

(c) the time at which or period within which the apparatus will be removed;

(d) the time at which or period within which the land will be restored."

Pursuant to Paragraph 40(7) of the Code:

"If the court makes an order under paragraph 44(1), but the operator does not comply with the agreement imposed on the operator and the landowner or occupier by virtue of paragraph 44(7), the landowner or occupier may make an application to the court for an order under paragraph 44(3)".

However, on an application either by Paragraph 40(6) or (7) of the Code, the Tribunal may not make an order in relation to apparatus if an application under Paragraph 20(3) of the Code has been made in relation to the apparatus and not yet determined.[11]

The nature of the various orders that can be made under Paragraph 44 are considered below.

Third Party Rights to Remove Apparatus

Paragraph 41(1) of the Code provides that the rights of third parties to require removal of apparatus under an enactment other than the Code, or right other than under an enactment, can only be exercised in accordance with Paragraph 41.

By Paragraph 41(2) and (3) the third party may give notice to the operator (in compliance with the notice requirements in Paragraph 89)[12] to remove the apparatus and restore the land within a specified period which must be reasonable.

Pursuant to Paragraph 41(5) of the Code, the operator has the right to serve a counter-notice within twenty-eight days stating either that the

---

[11] For which, see Chapter Four.

[12] For which, see Chapter Three.

third party is not entitled to require the removal of the apparatus, or specifying the steps which it proposes to take to secure a right as against the third party to keep the apparatus on the land.

In the event that the operator has given a counter-notice, the right of the third party to enforce removal of the apparatus may only be exercised pursuant to an order of the Tribunal.[13]

In the event that the code operator gave a counter-notice specifying the steps which it proposes to take to secure a right as against the third party to keep the apparatus on the land, the Tribunal may only make the order under Paragraph 41(7) if satisfied that the operator is not taking those steps or is being unreasonably dilatory in taking them, or that taking those steps has not secured or will not secure the right to keep the apparatus or to reinstall if removed.[14]

Paragraph 41(9) of the Code enables enforcement by the third party by application where it has the right to enforce the removal of the apparatus, either because no counter-notice was given pursuant to Paragraph 41(6) of the Code, or pursuant to a Tribunal order under Paragraph 41(7) of the Code. The third party can apply either for an order for removal of the apparatus under Paragraph 44(1), or enabling it to sell the apparatus under Paragraph 44(3).

Paragraph 41(10) of the Code provides that if an order is made by the Tribunal under Paragraph 44(1) of the Code, but the operator does not comply with the agreement imposed, the third party may make an application to the Tribunal for an order under Paragraph 44(3).

It should be noted that:

---

[13]   Communications Act 2003, Schedule 3A, Paragraph 41(7).

[14]   Ibid, Paragraph 41(8).

(1) An order made on an application under Paragraph 41 need not include provision within Paragraph 44(1)(b) or (3)(d) unless the Tribunal considers it appropriate;[15] and

(2) The right to seek an order under Paragraph 41(9) of the Code is without prejudice to any other method available to the third party for enforcing the removal of the apparatus.[16]

The nature of the various orders that can be made under Paragraph 44 are considered below.

Paragraph 42 of the Code governs the way in which Paragraph 40 of the Code applies when the third parties' right is the right to require the alteration of the apparatus in consequence of the stopping up, closure, change or diversion of a street or road or the extinguishment or alteration of a public right of way.[17]

A Separate Application for the Restoration of Land

Paragraph 43(1) of the Code enables a separate application to be made in the event that the condition of land has been affected by the exercise of a code right, and restoration of the land to the condition does not involve the removal of apparatus. Pursuant to Paragraph 43(2) of the Code, the owner of the freehold estate, the lessee or the occupier each have the right to require the restoration of the land in the event that the person is not bound by a code right.

This is subject to Paragraph 43(3) of the Code, which excludes the right to make an application in cases in which the land is occupied by a person who conferred a code right that is in force, and where that right entitles the operator to affect the condition of the land in the same way as mentioned in Paragraph 43(1), or is otherwise bound by such a right and

---

[15] Ibid, Paragraph 41(11).

[16] Ibid, Paragraph 41(12).

[17] A detailed consideration of these provisions is outside the scope of this book.

that right was not conferred in breach of a covenant enforceable by the relevant person.

In cases where the person has the right under Paragraph 43 of the Code, Paragraphs 43(5) and (7) set out that a notice, compliant with Paragraph 89 of the Code,[18] may be given to the code operator that specifies the period of the works, and that such period must be reasonable.

By Paragraphs 43(8) and (9) of the Code, in the event that agreement is not reached within twenty-eight days that the operator will restore the land, and the time within which the land will be restored, the person may apply to the Tribunal for an order pursuant to Paragraph 44(2) of the Code requiring restoration, or enabling it to recover the cost of restoration. If the code operator does not comply with an order under Paragraph 44(2) of the Code, the person may make an application for an order under Paragraph 44(4) of the Code.[19]

The nature of the various orders that can be made under Paragraph 44 are considered next.

Orders on Applications under Paragraphs 40 to 43 of the Code

Paragraph 44 specifies the orders which may be made by the Tribunal on an application under Paragraphs 40 to 43 of the Code.

Any order made under Paragraph 44(1) of the Code is an order that the code operator must, within the period specified in the order:

"(a) remove the electronic communication apparatus, and

(b) restore the land to its condition before the apparatus was placed on, under or over the land." [20]

---

18 For which, see Chapter Three.

19 Communications Act 2003, Schedule 3A, Paragraph 44(10).

20 Ibid, Paragraph 44(1).

Paragraph 44(2) of the Code confers the power to make an order that the operator must, within the period specified,[21] restore the land to the condition it was in prior to the installation of the apparatus.

Paragraph 44(3) of the Code provides for an order that the landowner, occupier or third party may:

"(a) remove or arrange the removal of the electronic communications apparatus;

(b) sell any apparatus so removed;

(c) recover the costs of any action under paragraph (a) or (b) from the operator;

(d) recover from the operator the costs of restoring the land to its condition before the apparatus was placed on, under or over the land;

(e) retain the proceeds of sale of the apparatus to the extent that these do not exceed the costs incurred by the landowner, occupier or third party as mentioned in paragraph (c) or (d)."

Orders under Paragraph 44(4) of the Code require that the landowner may recover from the operator the costs of restoring the land to its condition before the code right was exercised.

Paragraph 44(5) of the Code sets out that, on an application under Paragraph 40, the code operator may be ordered to pay compensation to the landowner for any loss or damage suffered by the landowner as a result of the presence of the apparatus on the land during the period when the landowner had the right to require removal of the apparatus but was

---

[21] In *Crawley BC v EE Ltd* [2022] UKUT 158 (LC), Cooke J declined to simply stay a reference for an order under Paragraph 44 of the Code where the code operator was trying to reach agreement with the same landlord in respect of a neighbouring site. She considered that doing so would go beyond the requirements of the Code, and instead ordered a specified period for removal of the telecoms apparatus of 6 months, which was suggested by the applicant.

not able to exercise that right. Paragraph 44(6) provides that further provision about this compensation is made under Paragraph 84(5).

Paragraph 44(7) specifies that an order under either Paragraph 44(1) or (2) takes effect as an agreement between the code operator and the landowner, occupier or third party that requires the code operator to take the steps specified in the order, and otherwise contains such terms as the Tribunal may so specify.

Summary

In summary:

(1) Paragraph 39 of the Code enables a landowner or occupier to ascertain whether apparatus is on land pursuant to a code right, and a landowner or occupier of neighbouring land may by notice require the code operator to disclose whether it owns apparatus over land;

(2) A landowner has the right to require the removal of electronic communications apparatus "*if and only if*" one or more of certain conditions are met as specified in Paragraph 37 of the Code;

(3) Paragraph 38 of the Code provides for the circumstances in which a landowner or occupier of any land can require the removal of apparatus. It refers to apparatus that "*interferes with or obstructs a means of access to or from neighbouring land*", which the Tribunal has determined refers to an extant, rather than potential or future, means of access. Importantly, the means of access must be extant at the time the Code Rights were conferred;

(4) The procedure for removal of apparatus is specified in Paragraph 40 of the Code and is triggered by service of a notice. If no agreement is reached within twenty-eight days of a notice being served, the landowner or occupier may apply to the Tribunal either for an order under Paragraph 44(1) of the Code, requiring the operator to remove

the apparatus, or for an order under Paragraph 44(3) of the Code enabling the landowner to sell the apparatus;

(5) On an application either by Paragraph 40(6) or (7) of the Code, the Tribunal may not make an order in relation to apparatus if an application under Paragraph 20(3) of the Code has been made in relation to the apparatus and is not yet determined;

(6) Paragraph 41 provides for the rights of third parties to require removal of apparatus in limited circumstances. Again, the procedure is by notice and the code operator has the right to serve a counter-notice within twenty-eight days stating either that the third party is not entitled to require the removal of the apparatus, or specifying the steps which it proposes to take to secure a right as against the third party to keep the apparatus on the land. In the event that the operator has given a counter-notice, the right of the third party to enforce removal of the apparatus may only be pursuant to an order of the Tribunal;

(7) Paragraph 43 of the Code enables a separate application to be made in the event that the condition of land has been affected by the exercise of a code right, and restoration of the land to the condition does not involve the removal of apparatus; and

(8) The Tribunal has wide powers pursuant to Paragraph 44 of the Code on any application under Paragraphs 40 to 43 of the Code requiring the operator to remove the apparatus and restore the land if the conditions are met. There is also power to direct that the landowner, occupier or third party may recover costs of taking such steps. Compensation may be ordered.

CHAPTER ELEVEN

THIRD PARTIES, CODE RIGHTS AND LAND REGISTRATION, AND THE ASSIGNMENT OF CODE RIGHTS

This chapter considers the following:

(1) Which third parties may be bound by code rights granted by others;

(2) How code rights interact with the Land Registration Act 2002 ("**the 2002 Act**"); and

(3) Code operators' ability to assign their code rights to third party operators.

Third Parties who can be Bound by Code Rights

Paragraph 10 of the Code takes effect where:

"a code right is conferred on an operator in respect of land by a person ("O") who is the occupier of the land when the code right is conferred."[1]

In those circumstances, there is a first class of third parties who are automatically bound by the code rights granted by O without the code operator having to take any further steps. These persons are set out in Paragraph 10(2):

---

[1]   Communications Act 2003, Schedule 3A, Paragraph 10(1).

"If O has an interest in the land when the code right is conferred, the code right also binds—

(a) successors in title to that interest,

(b) a person with an interest in the land that is created after the right is conferred and is derived (directly or indirectly) out of—

(i) O's interest, or

(ii) the interest of a successor in title to O's interest, and

(c) any other person at any time in occupation of the land whose right to occupation was granted by—

(i) O, at a time when O was bound by the code right, or

(ii) a person within paragraph (a) or (b)."[2]

And in respect of successors in title bound by a code right under Paragraph 10(2)(a), they are *"to be treated as a party to the agreement by which O conferred the right."*[3]

So, if O is the freehold owner of the land in question:

(1) O's (for example) assigns will be bound, and will be treated as a party to O's code agreement;

(2) If O (or O's assigns) grant a lease of the land to a third party, that lessee will be bound; and

(3) If O (or O's assigns) grant a licence to occupy the land to a third party, that licensee will be bound.

There is then a second class of third parties who are not automatically bound by the code rights granted by O, but can be bound if the telecoms

---

[2]   Ibid, Paragraph 10(2).

[3]   Ibid, Paragraph 10(3).

operator takes appropriate action. As set out in Chapter Three, Paragraphs 10(4) and 20(1)(b) Code provide that a telecoms operator can, after O has granted code rights to it, serve a Paragraph 20 notice on *"any other person with an interest in the land"*,[4] where the said land is already subject to *"a code right which is exercisable by the operator"*.[5]

So, where O is the lessee of a piece of land, the freeholder (and any intermediate landlords) are not bound by the code rights conferred by O unless and until they:

(1) Agree to be bound by them; or

(2) Are compelled to agree to be bound by them by the court, following service of a Paragraph 20 notice on them.

The former, simple agreement to be bound, is the means by which the first applicant code operator in *EE Ltd and Hutchison 3G UK Ltd v Edelwind Ltd and the Secretary of State for Housing, Communities and Local Government* [6] bound the freeholder to the code rights granted to it by the second respondent freeholder. The latter, compulsion under Paragraph 20, is the method which Lewison LJ suggested that Cornerstone bind Compton to code rights granted by Vodafone to Cornerstone in *Cornerstone Telecommunications Infrastructure Ltd v Compton Beauchamp Estates Ltd* at [89].[7]

Once a third party has been bound by code rights pursuant to Paragraph 10(4) of the Code, there is a third class of third parties who also become

---

4   Ibid, Paragraph 20(1)(b).

5   Ibid, Paragraph 10(4).

6   [2020] UKUT 272 (LC), considered in more detail in Chapter Eight.

7   [2019] EWCA Civ 1755. The Supreme Court's subsequent decision (which affirmed Lewison LJ's judgment for different reasons) is considered in more detail In Chapter Three, but does not undermine the correctness of Lewison LJ's suggestion here.

automatically bound by the code rights granted by O, which are set out in Paragraph 10(5):

"If such a person ("P") agrees to be bound by the code right, the code right also binds—

(a) the successors in title to P's interest,

(b) a person with an interest in the land that is created after P agrees to be bound and is derived (directly or indirectly) out of—

(i) P's interest, or

(ii) the interest of a successor in title to P's interest, and

(c) any other person at any time in occupation of the land whose right to occupation was granted by—

(i) P, at a time when P was bound by the code right, or

(ii) a person within paragraph (a) or (b)."[8]

And in respect of successors in title bound by a code right under Paragraph 10(5)(a), they are *"to be treated as a party to the agreement by which P agreed to be bound by the right."*[9]

So, where P is the freeholder of the land in question and O was P's direct lessee:

(1) P's (for example) assigns will be bound, and will be treated as a party to P's agreement to be bound by the same code rights that O conferred;

(2) If P (or P's assigns) grant an intermediate lease of the land to a third party, superior to O's lease, that lessee will be bound; and

---

[8]   Communications Act 2003, Schedule 3A, Paragraph 10(5).

[9]   Ibid, Paragraph 10(6).

(3) If P (or P's assigns) grant a licence to occupy the land to a third party, after the expiry of O's lease, that licensee will be bound.[10]

The Land Registration Act 2002

Usually, whether rights over registered land bind third parties is dictated by the workings of the 2002 Act. However, in respect of the Code, Paragraph 14 provides as follows:

"Where an enactment requires interests, charges or other obligations affecting land to be registered, the provisions of this code about who is bound by a code right have effect whether or not that right is registered."

So, code rights bind the third parties set out above without the need for them to be registered in accordance with the 2002 Act.[11] But this begs the question of how Parliament's intention that code rights need not be registered interacts is reflected in Paragraph 101 of the Code, which reads:

"The ownership of property does not change merely because the property is installed on or under, or affixed to, any land by any person in exercise of a right conferred by or on accordance with this code."

How the 2002 Act and Paragraphs 14 and 101 interact was decisive to the determination of one issue in dispute in *Cornerstone Telecommunications Infrastructure Ltd v Keast*.[12] In that case, Cornerstone sought to acquire code rights from Mr Keast over a small parcel of land

---

[10] P's agreement with the code operator to be bound by the code rights conferred by O will be a freestanding code agreement that will remain enforceable even after O's code agreement with the code operator is no longer enforceable against O (e.g. because O's interest in the land has extinguished and/or O's occupation of the land has ended).

[11] And the provisions of the Code about who is bound by a code right will simply have effect in respect of unregistered land.

[12] [2019] UKUT 116 (LC).

which already had a telephone mast and other equipment installed on it by Vodafone under the Old Code.

Mr Keast argued that Cornerstone was not entitled to the code rights it sought because:

(1) The Code regulates the legal relationship between code operators and occupiers of land;[13]

(2) Paragraph 108(1) of the Code explains that –

""land" does not include electronic communications apparatus";[14]

(3) The telecoms apparatus installed by Vodafone under the Old Code has become part of the land under the common law principles related to the annexure of chattels to land[15] notwithstanding Paragraph 27(4) of the Old Code, which mirrors Paragraph 101 of the Code –

"The ownership of any property shall not be affected by the fact that it is installed on or under, or affixed to, any land by any person in the exercise of a right conferred by or in accordance with this code";[16] and so

(4) By seeking code rights over the parcel of land in dispute, Cornerstone was in fact seeking code rights over telecoms apparatus, which is not permitted under the Code.

The first issue for Cooke J to consider was whether Paragraph 27(4) of the Old Code (and by extension Paragraph 101 of the Code):

(1) Merely prevents chattels, when becoming part of the land by annexure upon being affixed to it under the common law, from

---

[13] See e.g. Communications Act 2003, Schedule 3A, Paragraphs 3, 9, 20 and 105, as discussed in Chapters Two and Three.

[14] Ibid, Paragraph 108(1).

[15] [2019] UKUT 116 (LC) at [32].

[16] Telecommunications Act 1984, Schedule 2, Paragraph 24(4).

having their ownership passed from the telecoms operator to the landowner; or

(2) Goes one step further and also disapplies the common law rule that the chattels, upon being fixed to the land, become part of the land.

Cooke J's answer was reached by considering how the Code was intended by Parliament to interact with the 2002 Act. She found that:

"If part of an operator's ECA [(electronic communications apparatus)] on a mast site were to become land, albeit without a change in ownership, then the Code operator will not be able to sell that part of its apparatus without making a transfer by deed in accordance with section 52 of the Law of Property Act 1925, and on sale title to that ECA would be registrable pursuant to Section 4 of the Land Registration Act 2002. That would be an obviously absurd result and cannot have been part of Parliament' intention." [17]

Cooke J then determined that Paragraph 101 of the Code operates to disapply the common law rule that would otherwise see telecoms apparatus become land upon being affixed to it.[18] She went on to also find in favour of Cornerstone on the second issue of whether it could acquire code rights over the land in question:

"The prohibition upon the acquisition of Code rights over ECA does not mean that it is impossible to acquire Code rights over land where ECA is present." [19]

So whilst Paragraph 14 of the Code provides that code rights themselves need not be registered under the 2002 Act in order to bind third partes, the whole scheme of the Code is intended to work together to ensure that

---

[17] [2019] UKUT 116 (LC) at [44].

[18] Similar reasoning was adopted in relation to Scots law by the Lands Tribunal (Scotland) in *SSE Telecommunications Limited v Montgomerie* [2022] 1 LUK 568 at [23]-[24].

[19] Ibid, at [48].

no parties to code agreements are placed in a position where they are required to comply with any registration requirements prescribed under the 2002 Act in order for their rights, obligations or interests arising under the Code to be binding on third parties.

The Assignment of Code Rights

A code operator's right to assign the benefit of a code agreement that it has acquired from either O or P to another code operator is protected under Paragraph 16 of the Code:[20]

"(1) Any agreement under Part 2 of this code is void to the extent that—

(a) it prevents or limits assignment of the agreement to another operator, or

(b) it makes assignment of the agreement to another operator subject to conditions (including a condition requiring the payment of money)…

(4) From the time when the assignment of an agreement under Part 2 of this code takes effect, the assignee is bound by the terms of the agreement.

(5) The assignor is not liable for any breach of a term of the agreement that occurs after the assignment if (and only if), before the breach took place, the assignor or the assignee gave a notice in writing to the other party to the agreement which—

(a) identified the assignee, and

(b) provided an address for service (for the purposes of Paragraph 91(2)(a)) for the assignee." [21]

---

[20] Save that these provisions do not apply where the exercise of the code right conferred under the said code agreement depends on a right that has effect pursuant to an agreement that was entered into under the Old Code. See Chapter Eleven and Digital Economy Act 2017, Schedule 2, Paragraph 5(2).

[21] Communications Act 2003, Schedule 3A, Paragraph 16(1), (4) and (5).

Not only does this allow for a market in which competing code operators can freely trade their telecoms apparatus with one another, but it also facilitates code operators setting up joint ventures like Cornerstone. If Vodafone and Telefonica acquire code rights under the Code themselves, then they can subsequently agree to transfer the governing code agreements to Cornerstone for joint management of those rights without fear of this potentially uneconomical owing to the need to comply with potentially onerous conditions before being able to do so.

There is one condition, however, which is permitted:

"(2) Sub-paragraph (1) does not apply to a term that requires the assignor to enter into a guarantee agreement…

(6) Sub-paragraph (5) is subject to the terms of any guarantee agreement.

(7) A "guarantee agreement" is an agreement, in connection with the assignment of an agreement under Part 2 of this code, under which the assignor guarantees to any extent the performance by the assignee of the obligations that become binding on the assignee under sub-paragraph (4) (the "relevant obligations").

(8) An agreement is not a guarantee agreement to the extent that it purports—

(a) to impose on the assignor a requirement to guarantee in any way the performance of the relevant obligations by a person other than the assignee, or

(b) to impose on the assignor any liability, restriction or other requirement of any kind in relation to a time after the relevant obligations cease to be binding on the assignee.

(9) Subject to sub-paragraph (8), a guarantee agreement may—

(a) impose on the assignor any liability as sole or principal debtor in respect of the relevant obligations;

(b) impose on the assignor liabilities as guarantor in respect of the assignee's performance of the relevant obligations which are no more onerous than those to which the assignor would be subject in the event of the assignor being liable as sole or principal debtor in respect of any relevant obligation;

(c) make provision incidental or supplementary to any provision within paragraph (a) or (b)."[22]

This form of guarantee, stronger than merely being made surety, substantially mirrors the kind of guarantee that can be imposed under an authorised guarantee agreement under Section 16 of the Landlord and Tenant (Covenants) Act 1995. This guarantee should be some comfort to O or P, provided that they remember to insist that any code agreement that they enter into with a code operator includes the entry into of such a guarantee on any assignment (if this is not freely offered by the code operator in its Paragraph 20 notice).

Summary

In summary:

(1) There are three classes of third parties that can be bound by code agreements. The first is bound automatically, and includes assigns of, and those deriving interests or occupation from, the occupier. The second is bound only upon free agreement, or agreement being imposed by the court after service of a Paragraph 20 notice, and includes all those with an interest in the land in question. The third is bound automatically too, and includes the assigns of, and those deriving interests or occupation from, an individual from the second class that has become bound;

---

[22] Ibid, Paragraph 16(2), and (6) to (9).

(2) Code rights, whilst being rights that affect land, do not need to be registered under the 2002 Act. The Code is designed to ensure that code rights bind third parties unimpeded by registration rules; and

(3) A code operator's right to assign their end of a code agreement is protected from any conditions under Paragraph 16 of the Code, save that code agreements can require that code operators provide a guarantee in respect of the obligations being taken on by their assign.

CHAPTER TWELVE

THE TRANSITIONAL PROVISIONS

In this chapter we consider the transitional provisions between the Old Code and the Code set out in Schedule 2 of the Digital Economy Act 2017 ("**the transitional provisions**"), in particular:

(1) What are referred to in the transitional provisions as subsisting agreements; and

(2) The extent to which parts of the Old Code and the Code apply to subsisting agreements.

We do not consider the operation of the Old Code in any detail, as that lies outside the scope of this book.

Subsisting Agreements

The starting point in understanding the transitional provisions is to identify what it refers to as subsisting agreements, which are defined in Paragraph 1(4) of those provisions:

"A "subsisting agreement" means–

(a) an agreement for the purposes of paragraph 2 or 3 of the [Old Code]*, or*

(b) an order under paragraph 5 of the existing code,

which is in force, as between an operator and any person, at the time the new code comes into force (and whose terms do not provide for it to cease to have effect at that time)." [1]

And the time the Code came into force was 28 December 2017.

Subsisting agreements have effect from 28 December 2017 *"as an agreement under Part 2 of the new code between the same parties, subject to the modifications made by this Schedule."* [2] Similarly, *"A person who is bound by a right by virtue of paragraph 2(4) of the [Old Code] is, after the new code comes into force, treated as bound pursuant to Part 2 of the new code."*[3] The fact that subsisting agreements are treated as code agreements under Part 2 of the Code is key, given that (as set out in Chapter Eight) Part 5 of the Code applies to code agreements under Part 2. This is discussed in more detail below.

The Parts of Each the Old Code and Code that Apply to Subsisting Agreements

Whilst the Old Code has not been in force as a whole since 28 December 2017, the Code does not simply apply retrospectively to all subsisting agreements. The transitional provisions keep some parts of the Old Code in force as long as subsisting agreements exist.[4]

---

1 In *Vodafone Ltd v Gencomp (No. 7) Limited* [2022] UKUT 223 (LC) it was held that in order for an agreement under the Old Code to be a subsisting agreement it had to have been granted by the occupier for the time being of that land. And see below regarding the need for a subsisting agreement to be in writing.

2 Digital Economy Act 2017, Schedule 2, Paragraph 2(1).

3 Ibid, Paragraph 2(2).

4 Once the last subsisting agreement has come to an end, the Old Code will become entirely obsolete by virtue of it no longer being possible to enter into agreements under the Old Code and there being no subsisting agreements left to which any part of it is preserved to apply under the transitional provisions.

Code Rights and Persons Bound by Them

Notwithstanding that the Old Code is no longer in force, people remain bound by subsisting agreements:

"(1) A person bound by a code right by virtue only of paragraph 2(3) of the [Old Code] *continues to be bound by it so long as they would be bound if paragraph 2(3) of the* [Old Code] *continued to have effect.*

(2) In relation to such a person, paragraph 4(4) to (12) of the [Old Code] *continue to have effect, but as if in paragraph 4(4)(b) the reference to paragraph 21 of the* [Old Code] *were a reference to Part 6 of the new code."*[5]

So, the provisions under the Old Code in respect of rights to require the removal of telecoms apparatus do not apply to subsisting agreements. Part 6 of the Code applies to them instead.[6]

In respect of subsisting agreements, to the extent that parts of the Code (like Part 6) apply to them, references in the Code to a code right are:

"(a) in relation to the operator and the land to which an agreement for the purposes of paragraph 2 of the [Old Code] *relates, references to a right for the statutory purposes to do the things listed in paragraph 2(1)(a) to (c) of the* [Old Code];

(b) in relation to land to which an agreement for the purposes of paragraph 3 of the [Old Code] *relates, a right to do the things mentioned in that paragraph."*[7]

Assignment of Code Rights, and Upgrading and Sharing of Apparatus

Pursuant to Paragraph 5 of the transitional provisions:

---

[5] Digital Economy Act 2017, Schedule 2, Paragraph 4.

[6] For which, see Chapter Ten.

[7] Digital Economy Act 2017, Schedule 2, Paragraph 3.

"(1) Part 3 of the new code (assignment of code rights, and upgrading and sharing of apparatus) does not apply in relation to a subsisting agreement.

(2) Part 3 of the new code does not apply in relation to a code right conferred under the new code if, at the time when it is conferred, the exercise of the right depends on a right that has effect under a subsisting agreement."

So not only does Part 3 of the Code not apply to subsisting agreements, it also does not apply to agreements entered into under the Code if the code rights conferred thereunder depend on code rights enjoyed under a separate subsisting agreement to be exercised.

Notices Given under the Transitional Provisions

Pursuant to Paragraph 23 of the transitional provisions, any notices given under the transitional provisions have their content and rules for service governed by Part 15 of the Code.[8]

Notices and Applications for Code Rights under the Old Code

Paragraphs 11 of the transitional provisions provides that notices given before 28 December 2017 in order to acquire code rights under the Old Code will be treated as Paragraph 20 notices on any application made after that date. However, pursuant to Paragraph 12, where the application is also made before 28 December 2017, the application will be resolved under the Old Code but take effect as an order under Paragraph 20 of the Code.

Over five years after the coming into force of the Code, it is likely that these paragraphs of the transitional provisions are now obsolete.

Paragraph 13 provides that the coming into force of the Code does not affect *"any application or order made under paragraph 6"* of the Old Code, which relates to applications or orders for temporary rights under the Old

---

8   For which see Chapter Three.

Code pending applications for code rights under the Old Code. Similarly, this too is now likely obsolete.

Tree Lopping Notices and Applications under the Old Code

Paragraphs 18 and 19 of the transitional provisions work similarly to Paragraphs 11 and 12, save in respect of tree lopping rather than the acquisition of code rights.

Pursuant to Paragraph 18 of the transitional provisions, where a notice is given before 28 December 2017 under Paragraph 19 of the Old Code it (and any counter-notice given thereunder) will take effect under Paragraph 82 of the Code on any application made after that date.

However, pursuant to Paragraph 19 of the transitional provisions, where the relevant application is made under the Old Code prior to 28 December 2017, the Old Code will continue to apply to it instead of Paragraph 82 of the Code.

As with Paragraphs 11 and 12 of the transitional provisions, it is likely that Paragraphs 18 and 19 are now obsolete too.

Compensation

Pursuant to Paragraph 14 of the transitional provisions, the repeal of the Old Code does not affect its Paragraph 16 (dictating the circumstances where compensation was payable by a code operator under the Old Code for the exercise by it of code rights) or any other right to compensation in respect only of the exercise of code rights prior to 28 December 2017.[9]

Further, Paragraph 25 of the transitional provisions provides that, in order to avoid double recovery:

---

[9] See *Elite Embroidery Ltd v Virgin Media Ltd* [2018] UKUT 364 (LC) where a compensation claim brought under the Code failed where it should properly have been brought under the Old Code.

"A person entitled to compensation by virtue of this Schedule is not entitled to compensation in respect of the same matter under any provision of the new code".

These provisions will become obsolete once the relevant limitation period for such compensation claims has expired, if they have not become so already by virtue of there being no extant potential claims under Paragraph 16 of the Old Code (through Paragraph 14 of the transitional provisions) remaining.

<u>Continuation, Termination and Modification of Subsisting Agreements</u>

Paragraphs 6 of the transitional provisions is, practically speaking, likely the most significant provision contained therein.

First, recall that subsisting agreements now take effect as an agreement under Part 2 of the Code.[10] Second, that Part 5 of the Code applies to all agreements under Part 2 of the Code, subject to Paragraphs 29(2) to (4) of the Code.[11]

Pursuant to Paragraph 6(1) of the transitional provisions:

"This paragraph applies in relation to a subsisting agreement, in place of paragraph 29(2) to (4) of the new code."

Paragraphs 6(2) and (3) [12] of the transitional provisions set out that Part 5 of the Code does not apply to a lease of land in England and Wales if it is one to which Part 2 of the 1954 Act:[13]

---

[10] Digital Economy Act 2017, Schedule 2, Paragraph 2.

[11] Communications Act 2003, Schedule 3A, Paragraph 29(1). See Chapter Eight for code agreements that are not subsisting agreements.

[12] Paragraph 6(4) of the transitional provisions is not considered here as it relates only to leases of land in Northern Ireland.

[13] Landlord and Tenant Act 1954.

(1) Applies, granting security of tenure for business, professional and other tenants;[14] or

(2) Does not apply, only and so does not confer security of tenure, but only by virtue of an agreement to exclude that security entered into pursuant to Section 38A of the 1954 Act *and* the primary purpose of the lease is not to grant code rights (within the meaning of Paragraph 3 of the transitional provisions).[15]

Those with a good memory will recall that these replacement provisions apply slightly differently to Paragraphs 29(2) and (3) of the Code,[16] in that Part 5 of the Code does not apply to:

(1) Code agreements entered into under the Code with security of tenure under Part 2 of the 1954 Act whose primary purpose is not to grant code rights;

(2) Subsisting agreements that are leases with security of tenure under Part 2 of the 1954 Act; and

(3) Both Code agreements entered into under the Code and subsisting agreements, which are leases with security of tenure under Part 2 of the 1954 Act excluded under Section 38A, and whose primary purpose is not to grant code rights.

The difference being that if a subsisting agreement has security of tenure under Part 2 of the 1954 Act, it does not matter whether its primary purpose is or is not to grant code rights under the Old Code; Part 5 of the Code will not apply to it. The same may not be said for code agreements entered into under the Code that enjoy security of tenure

---

[14] Digital Economy Act 2017, Schedule 2, Paragraph 6(2).

[15] Ibid, Paragraph 6(3).

[16] For which, see Chapter Eight.

under Part 2 of the 1954 Act; whether or not Part 5 of the Code applies will depend entirely on the primary purpose of the agreement.[17]

The application of Paragraph 6 of the transitional provisions was an issue in dispute in the second appeal heard In *Cornerstone Telecommunications Infrastructure Ltd v Compton Beauchamp Estates Ltd*,[18] namely the dispute between Cornerstone, Ashloch Ltd and AP Wireless II (UK) Ltd ("**APW**"). In that case:

(1) Ashloch owned the freehold of a rooftop site. Part of the site was subject to an agreement between Vodafone and the previous owner ("**the Tenancy**");

(2) The Tenancy was for the installation of telecoms apparatus on the site, and enjoyed with security of tenure under Part II of the 1954 Act. Its contractual term expired in 2012, but Vodafone remained in occupation of the site thereafter;

(3) In October 2018, APW (a company that specialised in the acquisition of leasehold telecoms sites) took a ninety-nine-year lease of the rooftop site from Ashloch;

(4) On a date after the decision of the Court of Appeal in *Cornerstone Telecommunications Infrastructure Ltd v Compton Beauchamp Estates Ltd*,[19] Vodafone assigned the Tenancy to Cornerstone;

(5) Cornerstone then served APW with a Paragraph 20 notice, requiring it to enter into a new code agreement. Cornerstone did to because it considered that it was more advantageous to require APW to enter

---

[17] But it is not possible for code agreements entered into under the Code in the form a lease to enjoy both the benefit of Part 5 of the Code and security of tenure under Part 2 of the 1954 Act, by virtue of Section 43(4) of the 1954 Act. For those code agreements, security of tenure under Part 2 of the 1954 Act is excluded. See Chapter Eight.

[18] [2022] UKSC 18; [2022] 1 WLR 3360.

[19] [2019] EWCA Civ 1755.

into a new agreement under the Code than to seek a new lease under Part 2 of the 1954 Act; and

(6) APW argued that Cornerstone could not make use of Paragraph 20 of the Code to acquire a code agreement from APW, because It was the occupier of the site (making use of the Court of Appeal's erroneous reasoning in *Compton Beauchamp*). APW argued that Cornerstone's sole means of acquiring new rights over the site was under Part 2 of the 1954 Act.

Having decided that a code operator in occupation of the site is in fact entitled to apply under Paragraph 20,[20] the Supreme Court was open to Cornerstone being able to apply under Paragraph 20 in theory. However, it maintained that as the Tenancy was one which attracted security of tenure under the 1954 Act, Cornerstone could not apply for a renewal of its existing code rights under Part 5 of the Code. This raised the question of whether Cornerstone could apply for a renewal by novation of its existing code rights under Part 4 of the Code, where those same rights were ones it was precluded from doing (essentially) the same thing under Part 5.

The Supreme Court decided that it could, and should, not be able to do so as *"The Intention of the Government, following the recommendation of the Law Commission, was such that an operator should not get the retrospective benefit of the new Code".*[21] Lady Rose JSC explained that:

"It is open to Cornerstone to apply for additional code rights under Part 4 of the Code even though it is in occupation of the site. But it cannot bypass the fact that it has ongoing rights under a tenancy which it is entitled to renew— or bypass the terms of the renewed tenancy once it is granted—by applying in effect for modifications of those rights under Part 4... the paragraph 20 application is really an attempt to avoid the tenancy renewal route and to modify the existing code rights before Part 5 becomes available. It is right that the tenant should be in no better but no worse position that other operators

---

[20] For which, see Chapter Three.

[21] [2022] UKSC 18; [2022] 1 WLR 3360, [167].

with an agreement under Part 2. "[22] A correspondingly opposite result was reached in the third appeal heard in *Cornerstone Telecommunications Infrastructure Ltd v Compton Beauchamp Estates Ltd*,[23] being the dispute between On Tower UK Ltd and APW.

On Tower's telecoms apparatus was on the site pursuant to a lease that contracted out of security of tenure under the 1954 Act. It would have been entitled to apply under Part 5 for a renewal by novation, save for the unfortunate fact that its lease currently existed as an unwritten tenancy at will, and subsisting agreements must be in writing.[24] Given it did not have a subsisting agreement, it could not apply under Part 5 of the Code; and nor could not apply under Part II of the 1954 Act.

The Supreme Court found that On Tower was permitted to apply for a renewal of its existing rights by novation under Part 4, unlike Cornerstone.[25]

Some earlier insight was also given into the intended workings of Part 5 of the Code in the context of subsisting agreements in *EE Ltd and Hutchison 3G UK Ltd v Stephenson and AP Wireless II (UK) Ltd*.[26] Mr Justice Fancourt noted at [30] that whist Paragraph 30 of the Code provides for code rights to continue, where the agreement is a subsisting agreement this *"can reasonably be seen as a temporary position… rather than the basis for a continuing relationship."* The core reason for this being that where code rights under the new scheme of the Code are available to the

---

[22] Ibid, [169]. The Supreme Court went on to concede that it was unclear whether Cornerstone had applied for 'new rights' so-to-speak, or simply a novation of Its old ones that should have been renewed under Part II of the 1954 Act. It invited further submissions from the parties as to whether this issue should be reverted back to the Upper Tribunal.

[23] Ibid.

[24] Paragraph 2 of the Old Code required agreements made thereunder to be in writing. It follows that an agreement conferring code rights entered into before the Code came into force that is not in writing is not a subsisting agreement. See ibid, [50].

[25] [2022] UKSC 18; [2022] 1 WLR 3360, [165].

[26] [2021] UKUT 167 (LC). See Chapter Nine for a summary of the relevant facts.

code operator *"the prolonged continuation of pre-Code rights is not a satisfactory substitute for a new agreement, at least from an operator's perspective."*

Paragraph 7 of the transitional provisions then goes on to provide a few ways in which Part 5 applies differently to subsisting agreements:

"(2) The "site provider" (see paragraph 30(1)(a) of the new code) does not include a person who was under the [Old Code] *bound by the agreement only by virtue of paragraph 2(2)(c) of that code.*

(3) Where the unexpired term of the subsisting agreement at the coming into force of the new code is less than 18 months, paragraph 31 [of the Code] *applies (with necessary modification) as if for the period of 18 months referred to in sub-paragraph 3(a) there were substituted a period equal to the unexpired term or 3 months, whichever is greater."*

(4) Paragraph 34 applies with the omission of sub-paragraph (13)(d)."

So Paragraph 7(3) relaxes the date requirements in Paragraph 31 of the Code for subsisting agreements with short unexpired terms.[27] Perhaps more importantly, Paragraph 7(4) of the transitional provisions is designed to prevent the Tribunal, when considering what order to make under Paragraph 34 of the Code, from taking into account the consideration payable under an agreement whose consideration was fixed under the valuation principles contained in the Old Code, thereby preserving the sanctity of the new valuation principles set out in the Code.[28]

Objections to and Removal of Apparatus

Paragraph 15 of the transitional provisions provides that:

---

[27] See Chapter 8 for consideration of the date requirements of code agreements that are not subsisting agreements.

[28] For which, see Chapter Six.

"The repeal of the [Old Code] *does not affect paragraphs 17 and 18 of that code as they apply in relation to anything whose installation was completed before the repeal comes into force."*

Paragraphs 17 and 18 of the Old Code relate to the site provider's ability to object to the installation of telecoms apparatus installed wholly or partly 3 metres or more above the ground, and the code operator's duty to fix appropriate notices to said apparatus.

Paragraph 16 of the transitional provisions goes on to provide that the repeal of the Old Code does not affect Paragraph 20 of the Old Code (under which, *inter alia*, any person with an interest in the land or neighbouring land could give notice requiring the removal of telecoms apparatus *"on the ground that the alteration is necessary to enable that person to carry out a proposed improvement of the land in which he has an interest"*) [29] as it applies in relation to telecoms apparatus whose installation was completed before 28 December 2017.[30]

However, pursuant to Paragraph 16(2) and (3) of the transitional provisions:

"(2) A right under paragraph 20 [of the Old Code] *is not by virtue of sub-paragraph (1) exercisable in relation to any apparatus by a person who is a party to, or is bound by, an agreement under the new code in relation to the apparatus.*

(3) A subsisting agreement is not an agreement under the new code for the purposes of sub-paragraph (2)."

So, pursuant to Paragraphs 15 to 17 of the transitional provisions, where telecoms apparatus is fully installed on land pursuant to the Old Code prior to 28 December 2017, the provisions of the Old Code in relating to objection to or removal of that apparatus will apply. The sole exception

---

[29] Telecommunications Act 1984, Schedule 2, Paragraph 20(1) as in force on 27 December 2017.

[30] Digital Economy Act 2017, Schedule 2, Paragraph 16(1).

is that the Old Code's removal for redevelopment provisions will not apply where the relevant apparatus has since become subject to a code right under the Code.

In return for these provisions applying to telecoms apparatus installed prior to 28 December 2017, Paragraph 17 of the transitional provisions dictates that:

"Part 12 of the new code does not apply in relation to apparatus whose installation was completed before the new code came into force." [31]

Separately, pursuant to Paragraph 20 of the transitional provisions, where prior to 28 December 2017 a notice was given under Paragraph 21(2) of the Old Code requiring the removal of apparatus as of right:

"(2) The repeal does not affect the operation of paragraph 21 in relation to anything done or that may be done under that paragraph following the giving of the notice.

(3) For the purposes of applying that paragraph after the repeal comes into force, steps specified in a counter- notice under sub-paragraph 4(b) of that paragraph as steps which the operator proposes to take under the existing code are to be read as including any corresponding steps that the operator could take under the new code or by virtue of this Schedule."

However, as it is likely that no such notices given prior to 28 December 2017 remain unresolved, it is very likely that Paragraph 20 of the transitional provisions is now obsolete.

Parts 7 to 11 of the Code

Paragraphs 8 to 10 and 21 of the transitional provisions make provision in respect of those parts of the Old Code that correspond broadly to Parts 7 to 11 of the Code, which lie outside the scope of this book.

---

[31]   The application of Part 12 of the Code falls outside the scope of this book.

Summary

In summary:

(1) The transitional provisions deal with the parts of the Old Code and the Code that apply to subsisting agreements i.e. agreements entered into under the Old Code before 28 December 2018 whose term does not cease upon the coming into force of the Code;

(2) Persons bound by subsisting agreements continue to be bound by them notwithstanding the repeal of the Old Code;

(3) Whereas Part 3 of the Code does not apply to subsisting agreements, Part 6 does;

(4) Any notices given under the transitional provisions must comply with Part 15 of the Code;

(5) For the most part, notices given under the Old Code prior to 28 December 2017 take effect under their equivalent provision in the Code thereafter, but these provisions are now likely obsolete by virtue of nearly four years having passed since that date;

(6) Compensation payable for use of code rights prior to 28 December 2017 remains governed by the Old Code's valuation principles;

(7) Whether a code operator is able to renew their subsisting agreement under the Code or Part 2 of the 1954 Act is set out in the transitional provisions. These routes are certainly mutually exclusive, but it is possible for those who must renew their existing code rights under the 1954 Act to apply for new code rights under the Code; and

(8) Part 12 of the Code does not apply to subsisting agreements. Instead, provision is made for various rights to object to or require the removal of apparatus under the Old Code to be preserved in respect of apparatus fully installed before 28 December 2017.

CHAPTER THIRTEEN

PARTS 4A AND 4ZA OF THE CODE: UNRESPONSIVE OWNERS AND OCCUPIERS

This chapter explores the following:

(1)   The purpose of the new Part 4A of the Code;

(2)   Relevant land and the premises;

(3)   The request by the lessee and notice procedure;

(4)   Applications to the First-tier Tribunal;

(5)   Evidence;

(6)   The order, notice and obligations prior to the works

(7)   The works;

(8)   Ongoing obligations;

(9)   Assignment;

(10) Expiry and termination of orders; and

(11) Part 4ZA, its purpose and procedure.

Introduction to Part 4A

The Telecommunications Infrastructure (Leasehold Property) Act 2021 ("**TILPA**") was enacted to advance the policy of successive governments to provide greater access to fast, reliable and secure connections. It did so by introducing a new Part 4A after Part 4 of Schedule 3A to the Communications Act 2003.

The *Electronic Communications Code-Part 4A guidance* was published by the Department for Digital, Culture Media and Sport on 26 December 2022. This guidance explained that data provided by operators was that some 40% of their requests for access received no response and that, typically, operators by-passed such properties in order to avoid delays to the wider deployment. The effect was that residents of such properties missed out on superior connections such as the installation of fibre where there was only a copper line or connection altogether.

The government sought to address the problem arising from the failure to respond to access requests by operators through the new Part 4A. This legislation aimed to ensure that those in blocks of flats and apartments were able to access broadband services, as explained at paragraph 27A of Schedule 3A to the Communications Act 2003. The procedure was designed to create a "*streamlined*" [1] route to enable the operators to access blocks of flats and apartments if a service has been requested by a tenant but a landlord of connected land is repeatedly unresponsive. The intention was that the tenant would no longer be prejudiced by the silence of the landlord.

Applications are heard in the First-tier Tribunal (Property Chamber) ("**the FTT**") in accordance with Regulation 4(2)(a) of the Electronic Communications Code (Jurisdiction) Regulations 2017,[2] as amended by TILPA.[3] The Tribunal is preparing for a flood of applications in the first

---

[1]   As described in the *Electronic Communications Code-Part 4A guidance*.

[2]   SI 2017/1284.

[3]   TILPA, Schedule 1, Paragraph 8.

year these provisions are in force. It is anticipated that most applications will be dealt with on the papers.

Relevant Land and the Premises

Part 4A only applies to certain premises occupied under a lease, namely where the premises the operator is seeking to connect (i.e. the 'target premises') form part of a multiple dwelling building.[4] By s27I(1) of Part 4A of the Code, the interpretation section, a '*multiple dwelling building*' means a building which contains two or more sets of premises which are used as, or are intended to be used as, separate dwellings. For these purposes '*premises*' includes a part of those premises. The most common examples of a multiple dwelling building are blocks of flats and houses converted into flats. An order can be sought providing that the target premises are occupied under a lease and that the request for an electronic communications service is made by a lessee in occupation.[5]

Request by the Lessee and Notice Procedure

The process is triggered by the request from a lessee of qualifying premises that a Code operator provides their leased premises with telecoms services.[6] The operator then sends the *"required grantor"* (e.g., the freeholder) a request in writing to confer a code right on it.[7] This request is in the form of a Paragraph 20 notice. Please see Chapter 3 for the formalities regarding a Paragraph 20 notice.

By s27C(1) of Part 4A of the Code, the operator must serve two warning notices and a final notice before making an application to the FTT. The warning notice is defined as one which must be in writing and which

---

[4] Communications Act 2003, Schedule 3A, Paragraph 27B(1)(a) and 27B(2).

[5] Ibid, Paragraph 27B(1)(a) and (b).

[6] Ibid, Paragraph 27B(1)(b).

[7] Ibid, Paragraph 27B(1)(c).

includes a copy of the request notice.[8] The notice must specify which of the three notices it is and must state that unless the grantor responds the operator will be allowed to apply for a Part 4A Order. The notice must also set out the effect of the Part 4A order and contain any other specified information. Any notice which does not meet **all** of these criteria will be invalid.

The timetable for such warning notices is as follows. By Paragraph 27D(3) of Part 4A, the first notice may be given after the end of the period of seven days after request was made, beginning with the day on which the request notice was given. By Paragraph 27D(4) Part 4ZA, the second notice may be given seven days after the first notice, beginning with the day on which the first one was given.

Strict requirements regulate service of a final notice. By Paragraph 27C(6) of Part 4A, the final notice may only be given within the permitted period. The permitted period is defined in Paragraph 27D(7) and specifies the start date as beginning immediately after the end of the period of seven days beginning with the day on which the second warning notice was given, or the period of 28 days beginning with the day on which the request notice was given (whichever ends last), and ending at the end of a period of 28 days beginning with the day on which the second notice was given. The final notice must, together with the requirements for all of these notices, state that unless the *"required grantor"* responds within 14 days, the operator intends to apply for an order under Part 4A.

The following table may assist the reader in navigating this treacherous timetable:

---

8   Ibid, Paragraph 27C(2).

Notice	First Date for Service	Last Date for Service
Warning Notice 1	7 days after the date the request notice is given	N/A
Warning Notice 2	7 days after the date that Warning Notice 1 is given	N/A
Final Notice	The latest of (1) 7 days after the date that the Warning Notice 2 is given (2) 28 days after the date that the request notice is given	28 days after the date that the Warning Notice 2 is given

The Secretary of State may by regulations specify other conditions which must be satisfied before giving the required grantor a final notice.[9] By Telecommunications Infrastructure (Leasehold Property) (Conditions and Time Limits) Regulations 2022 ("**the Conditions and Time Limits Regulations**"),[10] prior to giving the required grantor a final notice the operator must satisfy certain conditions:

"*(2) The operator must inspect the register of title for the connected land under section 66(1) of the Land Registration Act 2002, and, if the connected land is registered, the operator must apply for an official copy of each individual register that includes the connected land or any part of that land under rule 134 of the Land Registration Rules 2003.*

---

[9] Ibid, Paragraph 27D(8).

[10] SI 2022/1057.

(3)   The operator must request that the lessee in occupation referred to in paragraph 27B(1)(b) of the code provides the operator with the name and address of the required grantor.

(4)   If the operator obtains new information regarding the name or address of the required grantor prior to giving the final notice the operator must withdraw the warning notices3 given under paragraph 27C(1) of the code and give the warning notices using that new information."

By Regulation 3(5) of the Conditions and Time Limits Regulations '*new information*' is new information regarding the name or address of the required grantor obtained by the operator which it reasonably believes is the name and address of the required grantor.

The Application

The operator is entitled to make an application for a Part 4A Order if the criteria in Paragraph 27D(1) are met. These are:

(1) The operator has satisfied the notice requirements set out in Paragraph 27C;

(2) The period of fourteen days beginning with the day on which the final notice was given has ended;

(3) The required grantor has not responded to the operator; and

(4) The operator has satisfied any other specified conditions.

A response from the grantor is defined in Paragraph 27D(4) of the Code as the required grantor agreeing or refusing in writing to confer or other be bound by the code right in the request notice or otherwise acknowledging in writing the request notice, a warning notice or the final notice.

The application must be made on notice to the required grantor.[11] The application must be made before the end of the specified period beginning with the day on which the final notice is given.[12] This is a period of 42 days pursuant to Regulation 5 of the Conditions and Time Limits Regulations.

Evidence

Regulation 4(2) of the Conditions and Time Limits Regulations requires that the operator must have retained for inspection by the Tribunal copies of the request notice, warning notices and final notice. The operator is further required to retain for the Tribunal's inspection:

"(a) evidence that each notice referred to in paragraph (2) was given in accordance with the relevant provisions of the code,

(b) evidence of a request to provide an electronic communications service to the target premises by a lessee in occupation under paragraph 27B(1)(b) of the code, and

(c) evidence of compliance with regulation 3."

Tribunal Procedure

The FTT's procedure is set out in the Tribunal Procedure (First-tier Tribunal) (Property Chamber) Rules 2013, supplemented with Practice Directions issued from time to time. For the purposes of Part 4A applications, the tribunal procedure rules were specifically updated in two ways.

First, provision was made for an *"unresponsive grantor case"*, which means *"an application for an order under paragraph 27D of Part 4A … of Schedule*

---

[11]   Ibid, Paragraph 27D(3).

[12]   Ibid, Paragraph 27D(2).

3A to the Communications Act 2003". [13] In such cases, an abbreviated procedure for paper hearings has been introduced. Ordinarily, the FTT may dispense with holding an oral hearing if (a) the parties consent, or (b) the Tribunal notifies the parties that it intends to determine matters on paper and none of them asks for an oral hearing within 28 days.[14] But in the case of Part 4A unresponsive grantor cases, that period has been reduced to 14 days.[15]

Secondly, amendments were made to rule 13 of the Tribunal Procedure Rules to enable costs shifting in cases involving Part 4A (Code rights in respect of land connected to leased premises) and unresponsive occupier cases.[16]

In 2023, the Senior President of Tribunals approved a *Practice Direction for applications under Part 4a, Paragraph 27d of The Electronic Communications Code* together with a Form ECC1 for use in the First-tier Tribunal (Property Chamber). Paragraph 2 of the Practice Direction states that any application under Paragraph 27D of Part 4A must be made in Form ECC1. Alternatively *"a form materially to the same effect and containing the same information"* may be accepted at the Tribunal's discretion. The form must be completed in full, and it must be accompanied by clear copies of certain documents specified in Section 16 of the Form. These are:

(1)   Proof of service of the application on the respondent.

(2)   The request for an electronic communications service.

(3)   Official copies of the register.

(4)   The request notice and evidence of service.

---

[13]   Tribunal Procedure (First-tier Tribunal) (Property Chamber) Rules 2013 rule 1.

[14]   Ibid, rule 31(3)(a).

[15]   Tribunal Procedure (Amendment No.2) Rules 2022 (SI 2022/312) rule 4.

[16]   Tribunal Procedure (Amendment) Rules 2021 (SI 2021/322) rule 4.

(5) The first warning notice and evidence of service.

(6) The second warning notice and evidence of service.

(7) The Final Notice and evidence of service.

(8) Evidence of compliance with regulation 3.

(9) A draft order.

The application form ECC1 applies to any application to impose an agreement on an unresponsive occupier of land. It must also be accompanied by a witness statement which is certified with a statement of truth, and which provides information confirming various matters:

(1) That the target premises are occupied under a lease;

(2) That the premises form part of a multi-dwelling building;

(3) That the connected land is in common ownership with the target premises;

(4) That the lessee in occupation has requested an operator to provide an electronic communications service;

(5) That the operator has required the required grantor to agree to confer a code right or otherwise to be bound by such a code right;

(6) That the operator has given the grantor the notices specified in Sections 8, 9, 10 and 11 of Form ECC1;

(7) That that before the final notice was given, an inspection had been made of the register of title;

(8) That before the final notice was given, a request was made of the lessee for the name and address of the required grantor and that new information was either not given or the warning notices were given using the new information;

(9) That the required grantor has not responded to the operator in writing at any time before the application was made; and

(10) That the Applicant will notify the Tribunal of any change in any aspect of the application, or if it receives any communication from the required grantor which occurs or is received at any time before the Tribunal makes its determination.

Three forms of evidence of service are approved:

(1) a certificate of service in form analogous to CPR Form N215 signed by the person who took the step identified in the certificate;

(2) proof of delivery from the royal mail or other postal service; or

(3) evidence, in the statement in accordance with paragraph 3 above, setting out the internal processes for sending of notices and the signatory's knowledge or belief that those processes were followed.

Failure to comply with the Practice Direction does not invalidate any step taken in the Tribunal proceedings: see Rule 8(1) of the Tribunal Procedure (First-tier Tribunal) (Property Chamber) Rules 2013 and *Lough's Property Management Ltd v Robert Court RTM Co Ltd.*[17] But the Practice Direction warns that failure to comply would enable the Tribunal to strike out all or part of their case pursuant to rule 8(2)(c) and 9(3)(a) of the 2013 Rules.

The Tribunal also publishes a Form ECC2 for compensation applications after the Tribunal has made an order. At the time of writing, this is not subject to any Practice Direction, and it is therefore an advisory form only.

A copy of the Practice Direction and Forms ECC1 and ECC2 can be accessed on the authors' Chambers websites.

---

[17] [2019] UKUT 105 (LC).

There is no guidance about other Code applications or any relevant application forms published on the Tribunal's website at the time of publication.

The Order, Notice and Obligations Prior to the Works

The Tribunal may make a part 4A Order *"if and only if"* it is satisfied that the requirements for applying for an order have been met and it is satisfied that the required grantor has not objected to the making of the order.[18] The emphasis makes clear that the formalities are mandatory.

A Part 4A Order is defined in Paragraph 27E(2) of the Code as one which imposes on the operator and the grantor an agreement by which the required grantor confers the code right identified in the request notice in relation to the relevant land.

The terms of the order made must be in accordance with regulations made by the Secretary of State [19] following consultation with operators, those who appear to the Secretary of State to represent owners of interests in land who are likely to be affected by the regulations, and any other persons the Secretary of State thinks appropriate.[20] These regulations must contain certain information as specified in Paragraph 27E(5) of the Code and must include specified matters now set out in regulations.

Regulation 2 of the Telecommunications Infrastructure (Leasehold Property) (Terms of Agreement) Regulations 2022 ("the Terms of Agreement Regulations"),[21] provide that the terms of an agreement imposed by a Part 4A Order are to be those set out in the Schedule. By Schedule 1, Paragraph 3(1) of the Terms of Agreement Regulations, before entering onto land in accordance with Part 4A rights the operator

---

[18] Ibid, Paragraph 27E(1).

[19] Ibid, Paragraph 27E(4).

[20] Ibid, Paragraph 27E(6).

[21] SI 2022/1232.

must give notice to the required grantor and each managing agent of the land or part of the land who is known to the operator.

Schedule 1, Paragraph 3(2) of the Terms of Agreement Regulations provides that the notice must contain certain information namely all details of the proposed works so far as reasonable practicable, the date on which works will commence and a reasonable estimate of the duration of the works and the name of the operator and an email address, telephone number and postal address in the United Kingdom at which the operator may be contacted about the relevant works:

The period of the notice is at least five working days before entering the land.[22] Service of the notice must be by a registered post service or by recorded delivery, pursuant to Schedule 1, Paragraph 3(4) of the Terms of Agreement Regulations. The operator must affix a copy of the notice, addressed to the required grantor and all residents of the multiple dwelling building of which the target premises are part, to a conspicuous object on the relevant land in a secure and durable manner in a position where it is reasonable legible. It should be noted that the requirements in Schedule 1, Paragraph 3(1) of the Terms of Agreement Regulations do not apply for entry solely to affix the notice under sub-paragraph (5), or where the entry is required solely for emergency works.

There is a requirement that the operator obtain consents, permits, licences, permissions and authorisations or approvals which are required to commence, continue and complete the relevant works by Schedule, 1 Paragraph 4 of the Terms of Agreement Regulations. This includes authorisation under Section 8 of the Planning (Listed Buildings and Conservation Areas) Act 1990, where Section 7 of that Act requires the operator to do so.

The operator must also indemnify the grantor. By Schedule 1, Paragraph 8(1) of the Terms of Agreement Regulations, the operator is required to

---

[22] Schedule 1, Paragraph 3(3) of the Terms of Agreement Regulations.

indemnify the required grantor against the indemnity liabilities [23] up to a maximum of £5,000,000. The grantor is required to give the operator reasonable notice of any indemnity liabilities, is required to mitigate the indemnity liabilities, and is prohibited from compromising or settling the indemnity liabilities without the consent of the operator.[24] However, the consent of the operator must not be unreasonably withheld or delayed. The grantor must also permit the operator to defend any claim arising from the indemnity liabilities in the name of the required grantor, but at the expense of the operator.

Further, by Schedule 1, Paragraph 9(1) and (2) of the Terms of Agreement Regulations the operator is required to have a policy of insurance with an authorised insurer [25] prior to entering onto the relevant land, and it must maintain the policy or equivalent cover so that it is able to meet the relevant insurance liabilities. These are liabilities in relation to death, bodily injury, or loss to any person or damage to property arising out of the exercise of the Part 4A code right. On a reasonable request by the grantor, the operator must provide the details of the policy of insurance or equivalent cover and evidence that it is in force.[26]

The Works

Unless works are emergency works, the operator may only enter the land between 8.30am to 6.00pm Monday to Friday unless varied with the written consent of a managing agent or recognised tenants' association

---

[23] Defined at Schedule 1, Paragraph 8(3) of the Terms of Agreement Regulations as "*any third party actions, claims, costs, expenses, proceedings or demands arising as a result of any act or omission by the operator in exercising its rights under this agreement or any breach or non-performance of the obligations of the operator under this agreement.*"

[24] Ibid, Schedule 1, Paragraph 8(2).

[25] Defined as "*a person lawfully carrying on insurance business of any class relevant for the purposes of the code, and issuing polices of insurance in the course of that business*" by Schedule 1 Paragraph 9(4) of the Terms of Agreement Regulations.

[26] Ibid, Schedule 1, Paragraph 9(3).

(as defined in Section 29 of the Landlord and Tenant Act 1985) relating to the relevant land.[27]

Schedule 1, Paragraph 6 of the Terms of Agreement Regulations places a number of obligations on the operator:

(1) The operator must take reasonable and proper precautions to avoid unnecessary or undue obstruction or interference with the entry on or use of the land or neighbouring land or unnecessary or undue nuisance;

(2) It must also ensure that the relevant works are completed in a workmanlike or professional manner with adequate and proper materials;

(3) The operator must also ensure that when the works are completed the nominated individual (being the person who the operator considers to be the most senior individual carrying out the relevant works) confirms in writing that the works have been completed to the standard required in Paragraph 6, Schedule 1 of the Terms of Agreement Regulations; and

(4) At the conclusion of the relevant works the operator must restore the relevant land to the reasonable satisfaction of the required grantor.[28]

The operator is required to attach a notice to at least one piece of the apparatus installed in exercise of Part 4A rights before the end of the period of three days beginning with the day after that on which the installation of the equipment is completed.[29]

---

[27] Ibid, Schedule 1, Paragraph 5.

[28] Ibid, Schedule 1, Paragraph 7.

[29] Ibid, Schedule 1, Paragraph 12(1) and (3).

Ongoing Obligations

The operator is under an ongoing obligation to maintain and upgrade the apparatus so far as possible to ensure that the apparatus does not cause any risks to the health and safety of any person including the residents of the multiple dwelling building of which the target premises are a part.[30]

The grantor is also under ongoing obligations in relation to the equipment as specified in Schedule 1, Paragraph 11 of the Terms of Agreement Regulations. It must not:

"(a)   damage, disrupt or otherwise interfere with the apparatus or its operation;

(b)   unreasonably obstruct, hinder or otherwise prevent the operator from accessing the apparatus or carrying out any activity in accordance with this agreement."

The operator is prohibited from preventing or inhibiting the provision of services by other operators to other premises in the multiple dwelling building save as necessary for the operator to exercise the Part 4A code right.[31]

Assignment of the Agreement

The operator may assign the agreement to a third party operator by Schedule 1, Paragraph 13 of the Terms of Agreement Regulations. There can be no assignment of the agreement by the grantor because Schedule 1, Paragraph 13 of the Terms of Agreement Regulations specifies that the agreement may "*only*" be assigned by the operator. The operator must ensure that a condition of any assignment is that the assignee must retain evidence regarding the assignment.[32]

---

[30]   Ibid, Schedule 1, Paragraph 10.

[31]   Ibid, Schedule 1 Paragraph 14.

[32]   Ibid, Schedule 1 Paragraph 13(2).

Expiry of the Part 4A Order

There are a number of circumstances in which a Part 4A code right ceases to be conferred on the operator or to bind the grantor as provided by Paragraph 27G of Part 4A of the Code. In summary, these are:

(1) If a replacement agreement comes into effect in accordance with that agreement;

(2) If the Tribunal refuses an application by the operator for the imposition of a replacement agreement, in accordance with that decision; or

(3) If the right has not ceased pursuant to paragraphs (1) or (2) above before the end of the specified period (which is to be no more than eighteen months, as specified in regulations to be made by the Secretary of State,[33] beginning with the day on which the agreement imposed by the Part 4A order comes into effect) then at the end of that period. That period is currently specified at 18 months under Regulation 6 of the Conditions and Time Limits Regulations.

A *"replacement agreement"* in relation to a Part 4A code right is defined as an agreement under Part 2 by which the required grantor confers a code right on the operator or otherwise agrees to be bound by a code right which is exercisable by the operator where that right is in respect of the same land as the Part 4ZA code right.[34]

The required grantor has rights in accordance with Part 6 of the Code to require the operator to remove any electronic communications apparatus which is on or under or over the relevant land when the code right has

---

[33] Communications Act 2003, Schedule 3A, Paragraph 27G(3).

[34] Ibid, Paragraph 27G(2).

ceased to be conferred on the operator or otherwise ceased to bind the operator.[35]

On termination under Paragraph 27G of the Code, the agreement terminates but the requirements for indemnification and insurance are preserved by Schedule 1, Paragraph 15(2) of the Terms of Agreement Regulations. These terminate when it is agreed in writing between the operator and the grantor that these rights should terminate, when a replacement agreement comes into effect, or no further indemnity liabilities or insurance liabilities may arise.[36]

Compensation

Paragraph 27H of the Code applies where the court has made a Part 4A order.[37] It confers power on the Tribunal, on the application of the required grantor, to pay compensation for loss or damage which has been or will be sustained by the operator as a result of the exercise of by the operator of the Part 4A right.[38] Such an application may be made at any time after the Part 4A order is made which includes after the code right has ceased to be conferred on the operator or otherwise to bind the required grantor.[39]

An order made under Paragraph 27H may specify the amount of compensation which is payable or give directions for the determination of any such amount.[40] The directions may provide for the amount to be agreed between the operator and the required grantor or for any dispute to be determined by arbitration.[41] The order may provide for the

---

[35] Ibid, Paragraph 27G(4).

[36] Schedule 1, Paragraph 15(3) of the Terms of Agreement Regulations.

[37] Communications Act 2003, Schedule 3A, Paragraph 27H(1).

[38] Ibid, Paragraph 27H(2).

[39] Ibid, Paragraph 27H(3).

[40] Ibid, Paragraph 27H(4).

[41] Ibid, Paragraph 27H(5).

operator to make payment by way of a lump sum, periodic payments, payment or payments on the occurrence of an event or events and there is a wide discretion to order that payments or payments are made in such other form or such other form as the Tribunal may direct.[42]

Paragraph 27H(7) of Part 4A notes that Paragraph 84 of the Code makes further provision about compensation in the case of a Part 4A order.

Part 4ZA of the Code

Although it is not yet in force, Section 67 of the Product Security and Telecommunications Infrastructure Act 2022 ("**PSTIA**") introduces a new Part 4ZA to the Code to be added after Part 4. It is anticipated that it will be in force shortly after publication and so consideration is given to this new part of the Code. It can be noted that the structure of Part 4ZA is very similar to that of Part 4A.

The aim of these provisions is to enable the Tribunal to impose agreements on non-responsive owners of relevant land in cases where the operator needs to install electronic communications equipment under or over relevant land, but does not need to install electronic communications equipment on the relevant land.

Paragraph 27ZC(1) of the Code provides that Paragraphs 27ZD and E apply where it is intended to provide an electronic communication service to relevant premises which require the installation of electronic communications equipment under or over relevant land but not on the relevant land. It is a requirement that in order to install and operate the apparatus that the operator requires a person, the *"required grantor"*, to agree to confer rights in respect of the relevant land or otherwise to be bound by such rights.[43] It is necessary that the operator has on or after the day on which Section 67 of PSTIA comes into force made a request notice in accordance with Paragraph 20(2) of the Code and that required

---

[42]   Ibid, Paragraph 27H(6).

[43]   Ibid, Paragraph 27ZC(1)(c).

grantor has not responded. A response is defined as being an agreement or refusal in writing to confer or otherwise be bound by the code right or otherwise to acknowledge the code request in writing

The provisions avoid an overlap with Part 4A of the Code. Paragraph 27ZC(2) provides that paragraphs 27ZD and 27ZE do not apply if the relevant premises are premises within the scope of Part 4A, which are occupied under a lease and the relevant land is connected land pursuant to Paragraph 27B(3).

"*relevant land*" for the purpose of Part 4ZA is land not covered by buildings nor used as a park or other recreational area, and land which is covered by buildings, used as a park or other recreational area and is of a description specified in regulations.[44]

The notice procedure is specified in Part 27ZD and requires two warning notices and a final notice. The information to be included is similar to that in Part 4A above, namely the request must be included and the notice must specify which order it is, explain the effect of it and include other prescribed information. The timetable for the notices is that the first may only be given fourteen days after the request, the second notice fourteen days after the first and the final notice between fourteen days beginning on the date of the second notice and ending at the period of twenty-eight days after the second warning notice.

Notice	First Date for Service	Last Date for Service
Warning Notice 1	14 days after the date the request notice is given	N/A
Warning Notice 2	14 days after the date that Warning Notice 1 is given	N/A

---

[44] Ibid, Paragraph 27ZC(3).

Final Notice	14 days after the date that the Warning Notice 2 is given	28 days after the date that the Warning Notice 2 is given

By Paragraph 27ZE, the operator may apply for a Part 4ZA order if no part 4ZA order has previously been made, the notice requirements have been satisfied, the relevant time periods have expired, the required grantor has not responded, and any other specified conditions are met. The application may not be made after the end of the specified period as set out in regulations and must be on notice to the required grantor.[45]

By Paragraph 27ZF of Part 4ZA of the Code, an order can only be made if the Tribunal is satisfied that the requirements are met and there is no objection by the required grantor. The terms of an agreement are those to be specified in regulations which are not yet available. However, the matters which the Act requires to be addressed in those regulations are very similar to those which had to be included in relation to Part 4A and so it is anticipated that the obligations will be similar to those relating to Part 4A Orders.

By Paragraph 27ZG a Part 4ZA Order expires if a replacement agreement comes into effect in accordance with that agreement, if an application by the operator is refused by the Tribunal or at the end of the period in the original agreement. At that point the required grantor has the right, subject to and in accordance with Part 6 of the Code, to require the operator to remove the equipment.

Where a Part 4ZA Order has been made the Tribunal can order compensation to be paid by the operator to the required grantor pursuant to Paragraph 27ZH of the Code. This can be in relation to loss or damage which has been or will be sustained and can be made at any time after the

---

45   Ibid, Paragraph 27ZE(4).

Part 4ZA Order has been made. The breadth of the powers to award compensation mirror those in Part 4A of the Code.

As far as Part 4ZA Orders are concerned, it is expected the FTT's procedure rules, Practice Directions and forms will be updated further to facilitate paper hearings and to enable costs shifting. Those further changes are expected to mirror the provisions for Part 4A Code applications.

Summary

In summary:

(1) This new procedure is designed to address the problem caused by non-responsive landlords;

(2) It applies only to premises which form part of a multiple dwelling building;

(3) The lessee triggers matters by a request to the operator;

(4) The operator must then make a request in writing and follow a strict notice procedure;

(5) It enables the operator to apply to the First-tier Tribunal for an order, on notice to the operator, only if no previous Part 4ZA order has been made, the operator has complied with the notice procedure and after that time limits in relation to that procedure has expired and if the grantor has not responded;

(6) The operator is under a series of obligations regarding the works and providing protection for the grantor and residents of the building regarding health and safety and damage to property;

(7) An order may be made if the grantor has not objected and the operator has complied with the notice procedure and the time limits have expired;

(8)   The terms which must be included in an order are as specified in the regulations;

(9)   The order may be assigned by the operator;

(10) Compensation is payable; and

(11) A new Part 4ZA procedure, where the operator needs to install electronic communications equipment under or over relevant land but does not need to install electronic communications equipment on the relevant land, is likely to come into force soon.

CHAPTER FOURTEEN

ADR, PROCEDURES
AND PRACTICALITIES

In this final chapter we consider:

(1) Pre-action engagement and ADR;

(2) How to commence proceedings;

(3) The response to proceedings;

(4) Statements of case;

(5) The timetable for determining applications;

(6) Directions;

(7) Evidence and hearings; and

(8) Costs

Pre-action Engagement and ADR

At the end of the T371 Notice of Reference, which a the form used in the Tribunal for cases including applications under the Code, there are notes entitled *"Guidance on Case Management Procedures"*. These notes include the following:

"*Alternative Dispute Resolution/Mediation*

The Tribunal supports the resolution of disputes by agreement between the parties. Information about mediation services …is available on our website or may be requested from the Tribunal. The Tribunal will usually delay determination of the reference where the parties wish to attempt mediation or other form of ADR."

Further, in the Practice Note[1] the Honourable Mr Justice Holgate referred to the requirement that the Tribunal resolve the dispute within six months and considered *"In view of this requirement pre-action engagement between the parties is strongly encouraged."* The Upper Tribunal Guidance clearly applies to applications under the Code, but it is anticipated that the Tribunal will be anxious to avoid delay in view of the tight and inflexible timetable and so the parties to a dispute should indeed, endeavour to engage in ADR prior to the issue of proceedings if at all possible.

Disputes under the Code are well suited to mediation. The flexibility of mediation enables a practical approach to dispute resolution which can avoid the need for proceedings. There are a number of specialist property mediators able to assist with these cases.

Other forms of ADR may also be used.

As referred to in earlier chapters of this book, the emphasis on ADR is increased by amendments to Paragraphs 20 and 32 of the Code by Section 69 of the Product Security and Telecommunications Act 2022 (**"PSTIA"**), albeit those provisions are not in force at the time of publication.

The Commencement of Proceedings

The procedure for commencing proceedings is governed by Part 5 of the Rules,[2] and as set out above the relevant form is the T371 Notice of Reference. Rule 28 provides as follows:

---

[1]   Practice Note: Electronic Communications Code.

[2]   Tribunal Procedure (Upper Tribunal) (Lands Chamber) Rules 2010, as amended.

"(1) Proceedings to which this Part applies must be started by way of reference made by sending or delivering to the Tribunal a notice of reference.

(2) The parties to the proceedings are the person making the reference and any person named as a party in the notice of reference.

(3) The notice of reference must be signed and dated and must state—

(a) the name and address of the person making the reference and, if represented,—

(i) the name and address of that person's representative; and

(ii) the professional capacity, if any, in which the person's representative acts;

(b) an address where documents for the person making the reference may be sent or delivered;

(bb) the name and address of any person named as a party other than the person making the reference;

(c) the address or description of the land to which the reference relates;

(d) the name and address of every other person—

(i) with an interest in the land or property; or (ii) in occupation of the land or property;

(e) the nature of the—

(i) interest in the land or property; and

(ii) the right of occupation;

(f) the statutory provision under which the reference is made (unless the reference is a reference by consent under section 1(5) of the 1949 Act);

> *(g) if the reference is made by a claimant for compensation or other monetary award, the amount claimed, an explanation of how that amount is calculated and a summary of the reasons for making that claim;*
>
> *(h) the matter on which the person making the reference seeks the determination of the Tribunal and a summary of the reasons for seeking that determination and, where the reference is an appeal under the Riot Compensation Act 2016, the grounds of appeal on which the applicant relies; and*
>
> *(i) whether the person making the reference wants the reference to be determined without a hearing."*

Form T371 contains those matters required under the Rules, including details of the person making the reference, of any representative, of the capacity of the person making the reference, and the form provides for a tick box choice (in so far as material to applications under the Code) between *"land owner/occupier; Electronic Communications Code operator; or other."* The Respondent's details and the details of their representative are required.

The Property to which the reference relates must be identified, including a description of the nature of the land (dwelling house, shop, vacant land etc.), the approximate area (if relevant) and the postal address. The statutory provision or agreement giving the right to refer the matter to the Tribunal must be identified, and in cases under the Code confirmation that the claim is under the Code. Details of every other person with an interest in the land, if known must be included.

The form requires information about arrangements for the hearing to be provided. The applicant is required to indicate whether it intends to call an expert witness, or more than one expert witness, although it is permissible to tick the box *"Unsure"*.

The applicant is required to confirm that the attached guidance has been read and to select between:

(1) The standard procedure (used in a case where a hearing is necessary and another procedure is not considered more appropriate);

(2) The special procedure (for cases of greater complexity, value or general importance or where there is another good reason for closer supervision of the Tribunal);

(3) The simplified procedure (for speedy and economical determination of cases in which there is no substantial issue of law or valuation practice and no substantial conflict of fact is likely to arise; and

(4) The written representations procedure (in which cases the Tribunal may direct that the reference will be determined without an oral hearing but will not usually do so without the consent of the parties.

In the event that the applicant has selected any option other than the standard procedure it is necessary to explain why the procedure selected is most suitable.

The Rules provide for certain material to be provided with the notice of reference. As set out at Rule 28(4)(a), a copy of the order or other documents in consequence of which the reference is made including any agreement conferring jurisdiction on the Tribunal. The form has a checklist for enclosures which is to be completed by the applicant.

Rule 28(4)(c) requires the person making the reference to provide the fee. The reference filing fee is £275 at the time of writing. The Tribunal's fees are available on its website, and the fees are as prescribed in the Upper Tribunal (Lands Chamber) Fees (Amendment) Order 2016.[3]

Rule 28(5) provides that the person making the reference must provide sufficient copies for every other person named as a party in the notice of reference of the notice of reference and documents listed in Rule 28(4).

---

[3]   SI 2016/434.

Rule 28(8) requires the Tribunal to send copies of the notice and accompanying documents to the person named in the notice.

The reference and documents can be submitted and tracked digitally online with the E-Filing service, or be sent to:

Upper Tribunal (Lands Chamber)
5th Floor
Rolls Building
Fetter Lane
London
EC4A 1NL

DX: 160042 Strand 4

Email: Lands@justice.gov.uk

Tel: 020 7612 9710 Fax: 0870 761 7751

The Response to Notice of Reference

Rule 29(1) requires the person to whom the Tribunal sends a copy of the notice of reference to, within one month of the Tribunal sending the notice, send or deliver to the Tribunal and the party who made the notice of reference a response.

Pursuant to Rule 29(2), the notice must be signed and dated and state whether the person making the response intends to take part in the proceedings. Information is also required including: the name address of the person and of their representative; the professional capacity of the representative; and an address for service of documents. The respondent must also provide a summary of their contentions,[4] and if the respondent is a claimant and the claim is for compensation or a monetary award, the amount claimed, an explanation of how that amount is calculated and a

---

4   Rule 29(2)(c).

summary of the reasons for making that claim.[5] The respondent is also required to state whether the person wants the reference to be determined without a hearing.[6]

Statements of Case

By Rule 29(3), after receipt of a response to a notice of reference the Tribunal must direct either that the parties must file and serve a statement of case or that the notice of reference and response to a notice of reference shall stand as the statement of case.

The Timetable for Determining Applications

Paragraph 97 of the Code refers to Regulation 3 of the Electronic Communications and Wireless Telegraphy Regulations 2011 ("**the 2011 Regulations**")[7] and records that this makes provision about the time within which certain applications to the court under the Code must be determined.

Regulation 3(2) of the 2011 Regulations require the Tribunal to determine applications for the grant of code rights within six months of receipt of the application. In the interim hearing in _EE Ltd and Hutchinson 3G Ltd v London Borough of Islington_ [8] the Tribunal described the requirement for the Tribunal to determine such applications within six months as an _"important feature of the Code…to resolve dispute without delay."_[9]

---

[5] Rule 29(2)(d).

[6] Rule 29(2)(e).

[7] SI 2011/1210.

[8] [2018] UKUT 362 (LC).

[9] Ibid, at [10].

In the substantive hearing in _London Borough of Islington_[10] Martin Rodger QC commented at [18]:

"..._That obligation is imposed in the public interest and is not one which either the parties or the Tribunal are free to dispense with. The Tribunal has interpreted the obligation as applying only to the acquisition of rights over new sites, and not to the renewal of rights over existing sites..._"

Albeit not yet in force, Section 72 of PSTIA will insert a new Section 119A into the Code that will allow the relevant Secretary of State to make regulations to provide that cases requiring the determination of questions under or in connection with the contents of the Code be determined within a specific period. It is yet to be seen how this power will be exercised, if at all.

Directions

Directions are likely to be given at an early stage in cases under the Code, particularly if interim relief is sought. The Practice Note [11] sets out that the first case management hearing in a dispute under the Code is likely to take place within two to three weeks of receipt of the notice of reference, and will usually be held on a Friday and if more convenient to one or both of the parties may be by telephone. In the Interim _EE Ltd and Hutchinson 3G Ltd v London Borough of Islington_ decision,[12] Martin Rodger QC gave directions on the day the application was issued.

The Upper Tribunal Guidance on Case Management Procedures provides a warning about compliance with directions as follows:

---

[10]   [2019] UKUT 53 (LC).

[11]   Practice Note: Electronic Communications Code.

[12]   [2018] UKUT 362 (LC).

"All cases – compliance with directions

Parties are expected to comply with a direction that has been given during the course of proceedings and non-compliance may result in a sanction being imposed. If you are unable to comply with a direction you must make an application promptly for an extension of time or for other variation of the direction(s) before the time for compliance has expired. See Rule 6 for full details of the interlocutory application procedure. You should seek the prior agreement of the other parties and, if it is not given, tell them that any objection must be made in writing to the Tribunal within 10 days. To make an application you must set out your reasons, confirm that you have given notice of the application to all other parties and enclose the fee for an interlocutory application. The fee is £110. Please note that all cheques must be made payable to 'HM Courts & Tribunals Service' (not the Lands Chamber)."

As recorded in the substantive <u>London Borough of Islington</u> decision,[13] by an order made on 22 October 2018 the Tribunal gave directions for the final determination. The code operator was required to provide an electronic draft of the agreement they sought and the relevant person was directed to return the draft showing any proposed amendments clearly marked on it. The code operator was then to respond to the amendments identifying those which were agreed or disputed. Finally, the parties were required to discuss the draft on a without prejudice basis with a view to narrowing the issues between them before filing the agreement in its final iteration together with a joint statement of the reasons for any remaining points of contention by 19 November 2018. The timetable was agreed. It should be noted that this requirement is likely to be included in most directions orders made by the Tribunal.

The respondent did not comply with the directions and relied upon a witness statement of its expert that explained in a narrative form the areas

---

[13]   [2019] UKUT 53 (LC), [15].

of disagreement. Martin Rodger QC considered that the "*respondent's disregard of the Tribunal's direction was deliberate*".[14]

The Deputy President referred to the time limit imposed on the Tribunal in such cases and continued:

"*The imposition of a time limit for the determination of references under the new Code means that an even higher degree of cooperation with the Tribunal and between the parties is required in these cases. The purpose of the Tribunal's direction for the service and completion of a travelling draft was to facilitate the discharge of its obligation to provide a decision within the 6 months permitted by statute.*

As this case has already demonstrated, the burden on the Tribunal's resources caused by parties who fail to cooperate with each other and with the Tribunal is considerable. The Tribunal had been invited to approach its decision on 19 October 2018 at the level of principle, on the basis that the parties would seek to reach agreement on the detailed drafting of the necessary agreement once it was known whether interim rights were to be imposed. Unfortunately the expectation that a sensible consensus could be achieved over the detailed terms of an interim agreement which was expected to last less than four months proved unjustified. The parties agreed virtually nothing and the respondent refused even to allow access for non-invasive surveys while terms remained unresolved. Eventually on 11 December 2018 it was necessary for the Tribunal to settle the form of the agreement, going through the draft document, clause by clause, selecting between the parties' rival formulations.

Before the hearing our expectation had been that part of the two days allotted to it would be devoted to argument on the specific terms of the final agreement which remained in dispute. Without a marked drafts from the respondent, or any document identifying its detailed alternative proposals, it was impossible for that exercise to be undertaken. The respondent appeared instead to anticipate that the Tribunal would resolve issues of principle … That was not the procedure the Tribunal had directed. Nor was it an acceptable

---

[14] Ibid, [17].

alternative, since the Tribunal is obliged to provide its final decision by 24 February 2019."[15]

The Tribunal rejected the submission of the relevant person that there was an issue of principle to be determined before further drafting could be attempted and continued:

"Where a party fails to co-operate with the Tribunal to such an extent that the Tribunal is unable to deal with the proceedings fairly and justly the Tribunal has power under rule 8(3)(b) of The Tribunal Procedure (Upper Tribunal) (Lands Chamber) Rules 2010 to strike out the whole or part of that party's case. We consider that the respondent's failure in this case falls within that description. The Tribunal cannot force parties to agree, but it can require them clearly to state their case so that it can identify and determine the matters in dispute within the time limit fixed by Parliament.

For these reasons we indicated at the start of the hearing that the respondent would not be permitted to call evidence or make submissions on the terms of the agreement (as opposed to the consideration and compensation payable). We exempted from that prohibition the issue of principle identified by Mr Wills, namely whether the Code gives the Tribunal power to impose a lease on the parties. As that is a question of jurisdiction it is necessary for the Tribunal to resolve it and it is to that issue which we turn first."[16]

Let this be a cautionary tale to any party in Code proceedings. Serious sanctions will be imposed for non-compliance with directions orders which are made.

Further, there is an obligation upon the parties to co-operate in enabling the Tribunal to meet the strict deadline imposed on it for determining disputes under the Code.

---

[15]   Ibid, [19]-[21].

[16]   Ibid, [23]-[24].

Evidence and Hearings

In addition to the case management powers in Rule 5, the Tribunal can give directions as to the issues on which it requires evidence or submissions and the nature of such evidence and submissions by Rule 16. Rule 16 enables the Tribunal to limit the number of witnesses and to direct the manner in which evidence and submissions are given including whether orally or by witness statement or written submissions.

Rule 18 provides that the Tribunal may, on the application of a party or on its own initiative, require any person to attend as a witness and to answer questions or produce documents in that person's possession or control which relate to any issues in the proceedings. If a person is subject to a summons that person may apply to vary or set aside the summons if they did not have an opportunity to object to it before it was made or issued and must do so as soon as reasonably practicable after receipt. A summons must give fourteen days' notice of the hearing or such shorter period as may be directed and, if the person is not a party, make provision for the person's necessary expenses of attendance to be paid and state who is to pay them.

The Tribunal may permit the parties to adduce expert evidence by Rule 16(1)(c). Any such expert evidence must be given in accordance with Rule 17. Pursuant to Rule 17(1), the overriding duty of the expert is to assist the Tribunal with matters within the expert's expertise, and this duty overrides any obligation to the party instructing the expert or by whom the expert is paid. Such expert is to be given by a written report unless the Tribunal directs otherwise.[17] By Rule 17(5) the written report must:

"*(a) contain a statement that the expert understands the duty in paragraph (1) and has complied with it,*

---

[17] Rule 17(4).

(b) contain the words "I believe that the facts stated in this report are true and that the opinions expressed are correct",

(c) comply with the requirements of any practice direction as regards its form and contents, and

(d) be signed by the expert."

Rule 19 provides that site inspections can be conducted by the Tribunal with the consent of the occupier to inspect land or property which is the subject of the proceedings and as far as practicable any other land or property relevant to the proceedings.

Withdrawal of the proceedings is permitted by and in accordance with Rule 20.

Costs

An award for costs under the Rules relates to the costs of the proceedings and is to be distinguished from consideration and compensation which are considered elsewhere in this book. Rule 10(6)(e) of the Rules provides that the Tribunal has power to award costs in disputes under the Code.[18]

In exercising this power, the Upper Tribunal in *Cornerstone Telecommunications Infrastructure Limited v Central Saint Giles General Partner Limited and another* [2019] UKUT 183 (LC), strongly warned against parties engaging in *"senseless disputes"* and *"disproportionate, inappropriate, and unacceptable conduct"*.[19] In that case, the Tribunal made only very limited costs orders in favour of the successful parties

---

[18] This marries with Paragraph 96 of the Code, which gives the Tribunal the power to award costs in code disputes where it exercises jurisdiction pursuant to regulations made under Paragraph 95(1) of the Code (which it does: see Chapter Four on Regulation 3 of the Electronic Communications Code (Jurisdiction) Regulations 2017 (SI 2017/1284).

[19] [2019] UKUT 183 (LC) at [2].

because none of them had covered themselves in glory in the way they had conducted themselves during the reference.

In _Cornerstone Telecommunications Infrastructure Limited v St Martins Property Investments Ltd_ [20] the code operator applied for interim code rights to acquire access and ancillary rights for making 'multi-skilled visits' to a site to assess its suitability as a potential site for telecoms apparatus. In this reference alone, the code operator's costs were £30,500.00 and the site provider's were £82,500.00. The Deputy President awarded the site provider (who was successful broadly as to the terms of the agreement to be imposed) just £12,500.00,[21] and gave the warning that applications for Interim code rights for 'multi-skilled visits' _"do not require extensive evidence... [or] complicated statements of case. They ought to be capable of being conducted within a relatively restricted budget"._[22]

Whereas most references will have costs determined under Rule 10(6), it is worth keeping in mind that Rule 10(1) also empowers the Tribunal to make an order for costs on an application or on its own initiative, but only in accordance with Rule 10(3) to (6). This includes:

(1) Its power under Section 29(4) of the Tribunals, Courts and Enforcement Act 2007 (wasted costs) and for incidental costs in applying for an order for such costs;

(2) If the Tribunal considers that a party or its representative has acted unreasonably in bringing, defending or conducting the proceedings; and

---

[20] [2021] UKUT 262.

[21] A similar sum was awarded to the respondent in _EE Limited v HSBC Bank Plc_ [2022] UKUT 174 (LC), which was resolved almost entirely by consent.

[22] [2021] UKUT 262, [44].

(3) In the circumstances in Paragraph 10(14) of the Rules, namely to pay the costs of an amount equal to the whole or part of a fee made which is not otherwise included in an award of costs.

Summary

In summary:

(1) Pre-action engagement between the parties is strongly encouraged and mediation is a good forum for disputes about the Code;

(2) Part 5 of the Rules govern how to commence proceedings, and in particular Rule 28 contains requirements which must be met;

(3) A party served with a notice of reference must respond within one month indicating whether it intends to take part in proceedings;

(4) The Tribunal can direct that the parties file and serve statements of case or that the notice of reference and response stand as statements of case;

(5) The timetable for determining applications is six months and there is no power to extend time. In these circumstances, the Tribunal is likely to be even more intolerant to a breach of directions order than would usually be the case;

(6) The Tribunal has broad powers to make directions;

(7) The Tribunal can control evidence at hearings including permitting expert evidence and site visits; and

(8) The Tribunal has power to award costs under its Rules, and has demonstrated that it will exercise its discretion in such a way as to disincentivise parties from 'over-litigating' simple issues, where appropriate. This is to be distinguished from the power to award payment of consideration or compensation under the Code.

INDEX

MORE BOOKS BY
LAW BRIEF PUBLISHING

A selection of our other titles available now:-

'A Practical Guide to Parental Alienation in Private and Public Law Children Cases' by Sam King QC & Frankie Shama
'Contested Heritage – Removing Art from Land and Historic Buildings' by Richard Harwood QC, Catherine Dobson, David Sawtell
'The Limits of Separate Legal Personality: When Those Running a Company Can Be Held Personally Liable for Losses Caused to Third Parties Outside of the Company' by Dr Mike Wilkinson
'A Practical Guide to Transgender Law' by Robin Moira White & Nicola Newbegin
'Artificial Intelligence – The Practical Legal Issues (2nd Edition)' by John Buyers
'A Practical Guide to Residential Freehold Conveyancing' by Lorraine Richardson
'A Practical Guide to Pensions on Divorce for Lawyers' by Bryan Scant
'A Practical Guide to Challenging Sham Marriage Allegations in Immigration Law' by Priya Solanki
'A Practical Guide to Legal Rights in Scotland' by Sarah-Jane Macdonald
'A Practical Guide to New Build Conveyancing' by Paul Sams & Rebecca East
'A Practical Guide to Defending Barristers in Disciplinary Cases' by Marc Beaumont
'A Practical Guide to Inherited Wealth on Divorce' by Hayley Trim
'A Practical Guide to Practice Direction 12J and Domestic Abuse in Private Law Children Proceedings' by Rebecca Cross & Malvika Jaganmohan
'A Practical Guide to Confiscation and Restraint' by Narita Bahra QC, John Carl Townsend, David Winch
'A Practical Guide to the Law of Forests in Scotland' by Philip Buchan
'A Practical Guide to Health and Medical Cases in Immigration Law' by Rebecca Chapman & Miranda Butler
'A Practical Guide to Bad Character Evidence for Criminal Practitioners by Aparna Rao
'A Practical Guide to Extradition Law post-Brexit' by Myles Grandison et al

'A Practical Guide to Equity Release for Advisors' by Paul Sams
'A Practical Guide to Financial Services Claims' by Chris Hegarty
'The Law of Houses in Multiple Occupation: A Practical Guide to HMO Proceedings' by Julian Hunt
'Occupiers, Highways and Defective Premises Claims: A Practical Guide Post-Jackson – 2nd Edition' by Andrew Mckie
'A Practical Guide to Financial Ombudsman Service Claims' by Adam Temple & Robert Scrivenor
'A Practical Guide to Advising Schools on Employment Law' by Jonathan Holden
'A Practical Guide to Running Housing Disrepair and Cavity Wall Claims: 2nd Edition' by Andrew Mckie & Ian Skeate
'A Practical Guide to Holiday Sickness Claims – 2nd Edition' by Andrew Mckie & Ian Skeate
'Arguments and Tactics for Personal Injury and Clinical Negligence Claims' by Dorian Williams
'A Practical Guide to Drone Law' by Rufus Ballaster, Andrew Firman, Eleanor Clot
'A Practical Guide to Compliance for Personal Injury Firms Working With Claims Management Companies' by Paul Bennett
'RTA Allegations of Fraud in a Post-Jackson Era: The Handbook – 2nd Edition' by Andrew Mckie
'RTA Personal Injury Claims: A Practical Guide Post-Jackson' by Andrew Mckie
'On Experts: CPR35 for Lawyers and Experts' by David Boyle
'An Introduction to Personal Injury Law' by David Boyle

These books and more are available to order online direct from the publisher at www.lawbriefpublishing.com, where you can also read free sample chapters. For any queries, contact us on 0844 587 2383 or mail@lawbriefpublishing.com.

Our books are also usually in stock at www.amazon.co.uk with free next day delivery for Prime members, and at good legal bookshops such as Wildy & Sons.

We are regularly launching new books in our series of practical day-to-day practitioners' guides. Visit our website and join our free newsletter to be kept informed and to receive special offers, free chapters, etc.

You can also follow us on Twitter at www.twitter.com/lawbriefpub.